Collage Playground

A Fresh Approach to Creating Mixed-Media Art

kimberly santiago

NORTH LIGHT BOOKS

CINCINNATI, OHIO

14 13 12 11   5 4 3

Distributed in Canada by Fraser Direct
100 Armstrong Avenue
Georgetown, ON, Canada L7G 5S4
Tel: (905) 877-4411
Distributed in the U.K. and Europe by David & Charles
Brunel House, Newton Abbot, Devon, TQ12 4PU, England
Tel: (+44) 1626 323200, Fax: (+44) 1626 323319
E-mail: postmaster@davidandcharles.co.uk

Distributed in Australia by Capricorn Link
P.O. Box 704, S. Windsor, NSW 2756 Australia
Tel: (02) 4577-3555

Library of Congress Cataloging-in-Publication Data
Santiago, Kimberly.
  Collage playground : a fresh approach to creating mixed-media art / by Kimberly Santiago.
    p. cm.
  Includes index.
  ISBN 978-1-60061-793-5 (pbk. : alk. paper)
  1. Collage. 2. Collage--Technique. I. Title.
TT910.S26 2010
702.81'2--dc22
                                    2009049807

A Note About Copyright-Free Images

The projects in this book employ the use of photocopied images. Please ensure that the images you use are either your own, or copyright-free. Copyright-free means that the copyright has expired on the image, or that the image is free for anyone to use without permission.

METRIC CONVERSION CHART

TO CONVERT	TO	MULTIPLY BY
Inches	Centimeters	2.54
Centimeters	Inches	0.4
Feet	Centimeters	30.5
Centimeters	Feet	0.03
Yards	Meters	0.9
Meters	Yards	1.1
Sq. Inches	Sq. Centimeters	6.45
Sq. Centimeters	Sq. Inches	0.16
Sq. Feet	Sq. Meters	0.09
Sq. Meters	Sq. Feet	10.8
Sq. Yards	Sq. Meters	0.8
Sq. Meters	Sq. Yards	1.2
Pounds	Kilograms	0.45
Kilograms	Pounds	2.2
Ounces	Grams	28.3
Grams	Ounces	0.035

Editor: Julie Hollyday
Designer: Julie Barnett and Kelly O'Dell
Production Coordinator: Greg Nock
Photographer: Christine Polomsky
Photo Stylist: Julie Barnett

fw media
www.fwmedia.com

Dedication

This book is dedicated to my husband, Luis, the man who stands with me on this journey of life, and to our two daughters, Brittney and Amber, our finest creations.

A special dedication to my twin brother, Keith, for his lifetime of encouragement. To my father, who lost his fight with cancer before the book was finished; his strength has carried me through.

Believe in yourself and others will too.

Acknowledgments

Art is a statement of who we are and what we have experienced. I am fortunate to see life through many different eyes. I am especially grateful to be surrounded by wonderful friends and family whose contributions to my art have been my lifeline. To my two sons-in-law: Ian, for dragging home "collage resources" every time he left the country, and Justin, for answering my computer questions. To my dear friends, who continually give me ephemera to make my art. Their words of sincerity and support helped me make it through difficult times.

To artists everywhere, thank you for your expressions of life. My hope is that you read this book and continue to grow and make art.

To the people "behind the scenes"—because, without them, none of this is possible. To my editor, Julie Hollyday, who is always one step ahead of me. To the talented and ever-kind Christine Polomsky. To the person who opened the door, Tonia Davenport: thank you for giving me this incredible opportunity. To Christine Doyle, for always being available. To the designers of this book, Kelly O'Dell and Julie Barnett: thank you both for making it all fall into place. To the other members of the North Light family: a heartfelt thank you—your work and dedication are greatly appreciated.

About Kimberly

Kimberly Santiago began her career as a graphic designer and was elated to be recognized in the *HOW* design magazine self-promotion issue. She continued to work in the design field and win other awards—notably, Conqueror Paper Design Competition, for which her work was exhibited in London at Wiggins Teape Paperpoint Gallery, the Design Museum at Butler's Wharf and, later, in a Paris venue. From graphic design, she metamorphosed into an instructor and later the Department Chair of Graphic Design and Fine Art at O'More College of Design. She continues teaching art in workshops and private settings.

Always experimenting with new techniques and developing her artwork, Kimberly's interest is concentrated in collage. The desire to create art, deconstruct it and then reconstruct it, grips her soul.

She is currently living in Clarksville, Tennessee, with her husband, Luis, the love of her life. She has two beautiful daughters and two wonderful grandchildren.

Her perfect day is to be in her home studio working on art with her trusty assistant (and cat) Boo Boo Kitty, create until she is exhausted, take a nap and start all over again.

Photo by Becky Hall

Table
of
Contents

Introduction

Think of your school days and how you could not wait until it was time for recess. Once again, the playground is beckoning you—the swings are still and the slide and merry-go-round are all waiting for you to bring it on. Come out, let's play and make some art.

Collage is similar to a playground because it's user-friendly and accessible to people of all ages and skill levels. The equipment is equally as friendly, often items you already have in your household. I think this is what makes this medium so rewarding. Collage is layering and uncovering ideas, a continuum of thoughts. As each collage evolves, it becomes a metamorphosis of art.

Ever had one of those days where you overthink everything? The right side of your brain is telling you to create, and the left side of your brain is saying, "Now let's sit down and ponder this idea." I have a solution for you: just go with creativity. Find your inner child and let loose with your art. Pull out those unfinished drawings, paintings and sketches; grab that box of loose photos and paper scraps; leaf through old books, magazines and textiles.

That's right, go back to the playground! The place you ran around, free of your inhibitions. Go back to the stories you would make up and the drawings that went with them. Go back to your wide-open imagination and just create.

I hope this book will give you the tools to help free your imagination so you can see all the possibilities of your art. Take these techniques and make them your own with your favorite images, colors and media. Make art that speaks to your inner creative soul and you'll have art to cherish.

Join me on the playground, and let's have some fun!

bird

CHAPTER ONE

Getting Ready to Play

Even as an adult, I continue to purchase "back to school" supplies. Who can resist the penny pencils, fifty-cent composition books and bargain-basement loose-leaf paper? I love to look through the folders and notebooks to see what the "cool kids" will be buying. I always come across some item I can't walk away from, knowing it will make my life easier or at least more fun.

This chapter is all about collecting and organizing your supplies. The items mentioned here are the essential raw materials you'll need for your Collage Toy Box. Each time you create a collage or mixed-media piece of art, you'll need an adhesive, a support, surface-enriching media and collage resources. In Chapter Two, I'll show you how to take some of these raw materials and turn them into Collage Elements—fun items to have on hand to help preserve the images you love the most so you can use them in multiple ways.

So let's jump in to the sandbox, dig around and see what we come up with!

The Collage Toy Box

You will find there are certain supplies you reach for over and over again. To help ease the time spent searching and gathering these supplies for every project, I have organized a one-stop spot: the Collage Toy Box.

The Collage Toy Box contains all the supplies necessary to create a piece of collage art. Having everything in a container helps keep your supplies in one easy location and convenient to transport.

Take the time to create your Collage Toy Box to be ready for every project. Be creative when selecting your container; look for something that is sturdy and portable. Think about using a small vintage suitcase, cigar box or a photo storage box. Take it a step further and personalize the outside of your Collage Toy Box and then add your favorite toys!

Tip

To ensure safety, always follow the manufacturer's instructions and safety guidelines for products used in this book.

Adhesives

Selecting an adhesive is primarily based on the type of materials involved in the collage. Each manufacturer will list the materials that work well with their product; I recommend taking the time to understand the qualities of each product you use. Tinker around with your adhesives to see how they work for you!

What make things stick together? Let's take a look at different adhesives.

Matte Medium

This acrylic emulsion dries clear and is water based, which means it can be diluted with water. It is a good adhesive for paper, lightweight materials and small embellishments.

Rubber Cement

This adhesive works well with papers, especially Color-aid paper, because it resists bubbling and buckling. You may substitute Double Tack Mounting Film in place of rubber cement.

Double Tack Mounting Film

This double-sided adhesive film made by Grafix can turn anything into a sticker. It is a strong, heat-resistant, acid-free, permanent adhesive that cuts easily and bonds instantly.

Fusible Webbing

This is a paper-backed adhesive web that bonds two materials together. It is recommended for fabric, but I also use it on paper. This product will fuse fabric to fabric or other porous surfaces. It comes in different weights, to be used according to the weight of the materials being bonded. I used the light or medium weight for the projects in this book.

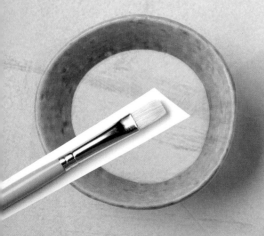

Two-Sided Tape

Use two-sided tape in small coverage areas or for interactive purposes. I use two-sided tape to hold strips of paper when weaving (see page 28).

Glue Stick

Glue sticks are clean and easy to use. I like to use glue sticks when creating Collage Elements, especially Collage Sheets (see page 18). This adhesive is quick and easy to dispense and is great for paper and lightweight materials.

Self-Adhesive Foam Pop-Ups

These thick, double-sided adhesives can help add dimension to your art work. You can find these in different sizes and shapes along with the scrapbooking supplies.

Supports

Supports are the surfaces on which collages are built. Selecting a support is a vital decision when creating a collage. Things to consider are the weights of the items being added, the types of adhesive used to apply the collage items and which surface-enriching media will be used in the collage. It is important to know how your support material will react to each one of these factors. For example, let's say you select to collage with paper and enrich the surface with paint. You must choose a support that will accept a wet medium. The support also needs to be strong and sturdy enough not to bow under the weight of the materials.

Self-Adhesive Mounting Board

These boards make quick work of adding lightweight backgrounds to your art: Simply lay the paper, fabric or other lightweight (preferably flat and smooth) material over the surface and smooth it out with your hand. You can then use other mediums and adhesives to build your collage. You should cover the entire surface of the board, or you might get something you didn't intend stuck onto your artwork!

Chipboard

This inexpensive support material is available in different thicknesses and sizes. It is very porous, which means it is highly absorbent. I have found that it works great if you use fusible webbing to iron paper directly on the chipboard. If you are using matte medium, it is best to prime the chipboard with acrylic paint, allow the paint to dry and then apply the matte medium. To prevent the board from buckling, place the board on a flat surface, add a weight on top and allow to dry.

Foamcore Board

An inexpensive support material, foamcore board is lightweight and easy to cut. This support is highly compatible with Double Tack Mounting Film, lightweight materials and minimal layering.

Stretched Canvas

Coated with gesso, stretched canvas works well with matte medium, light- to medium-weight materials and medium to heavy layering. Canvas is also good for the decollage technique (see pages 100–101).

Bristol Board, Illustration Board and Watercolor Paper

Bristol board and other similar boards such as watercolor paper and illustration board are inexpensive support materials. These boards work well with the majority of adhesives and can handle a lot of layering. To prevent the board from buckling, place it on a flat surface, add a weight on top and allow to dry.

Wood

Wood provides a very strong surface for all materials and weights. Raw wood is porous; therefore matte medium is an excellent choice as an adhesive.

a light coat on vintage book pages. The paint dries to a clear finish, letting the text of the book page show through. Spend some time with different spray-paint finishes. Remember to read all manufacturer instructions and warnings.

Oil Pastels

The rich colors of oil pastels blend and mix well on most surfaces and provide beautiful textural quality. I recommend a box of twenty-four colors to give you lots of options to play with.

Permanent Markers

Permanent markers come in different colors and tip sizes. They are perfect to emphasize an image in a collage, write with or outline shapes. Black permanent markers with tips ranging from extra-fine to medium can be extremely useful in collage work. An assortment of colors lets you punch up the color of any piece of art or add color where you feel it's needed.

Colored Pencils

You may purchase colored pencils individually or in different sets. I recommend a set of twelve, including black and white. If you find you need more colors, you may add to your set. Colored pencils are applied to dry, porous surfaces.

Rubber Stamps and Ink Pads

Artistically designed stamps are readily available for purchase in art and craft stores. You also have the option to make your own rubber stamps. Look for rubber-stamp kits, composed of self-adhesive rubber sheets and wood blocks. To make a stamp,

Surface-Enriching Media

Surface-enriching media are products used to enhance your collage. They can be used on materials before you adhere them to your collage or after the materials have been affixed to the art. You may also use these materials directly on the support—for example, painting a canvas before applying collage material.

Acrylic Paints

These water-based paints become transparent when mixed with matte medium. They may be purchased in an array of colors, or you may mix your own. I recommend getting a set of twelve colors, including black and white, for a great set of choices.

Watercolors

Available in tubes, liquids, pencils or cakes, watercolors are easy to use and clean up. Pencils offer the most control, with liquids being the most saturated (full of color).

Spray Paints

Fun to experiment with when developing Collage Elements, spray paints are available in many colors and for many types of surfaces. I like to use transparent spray paint, which is made for glass. I spray

draw on the paper backing of the sheet, cut out the design with scissors and adhere it to a wood block. Then ink up the rubber stamp and stamp away!

Gesso
This pigment is perfect for priming canvas and other porous materials. Brush on gesso with a flat brush, allow to dry and begin your artistic creation.

Rub-On Transfers
Traditionally a scrapbooking and cardmaking supply, rub-on transfers can add another layer of detail to your art without any bulk. I'll teach you how to make your own by using a product called "Rub-onz" by Grafix (see page 32). This material may be purchased at most art and craft stores or online.

Stickers
Stickers can instantly change the appearance of a collage. You will have the opportunity to create a sheet of your own art on sticker paper (page 33).

Transparency Adhesive Sheets
These sheets are perfect for layering. In the project *Bandana* (see page 108) you will see the full value of having art printed on a transparency sheet.

Collage Resources

I loved show-and-tell day at school; I felt it was the time I got to know myself as well as others. I take this same view of the materials people select for their Collage Resources—the papers, maps, stamps, pamphlets, brochures and photos. What is it that appeals to you? Is there a common thread, or is it just a random selection?

Collage sources are abundant and found everywhere. Unsure of what to look for? Get started by looking over the list below and then select what appeals to you—just like show-and-tell.

- Vintage books, pages and book jackets
- Maps, graphs and charts
- Postage stamps and collectible handbills
- Postcards, letters, cards and mail labels

- Advertisements, brochures and pamphlets
- Newspapers
- Kraft paper, gift bags and retail bags
- Vellum, decorative and scrapbook papers
- Food product packaging, cereal boxes, bags and food labels
- Old prints, paintings, sketches and unfinished art
- Signs, posters and catalog pages
- Purchased papers, tissue paper and wrapping paper
- Stencil templates
- Vintage textiles, handkerchiefs, doilies and tablecloths

Hide-and-Seek
Collage Resources are Everywhere You Look!

If you do not already have a box full of collage resources, cast your eye to some of the everyday items you don't normally give a second look—you'll be amazed at how much is hiding in plain sight!

There is no need to leave your house. I am sure you have plenty of collage resources at your fingertips. Do you get junk mail? Do you have wrapping paper? What about an old book?

If you want to venture out of your home, visit a flea market, antiques store, thrift store or, better yet, a friend's house. Try this little challenge: Take a walk, pick up ten items and make a piece of art.

I am fortunate in that my friends know my attraction to collage resources, and they are always donating to my cause. Put the word out; I bet you will be pleased at what your friends give you.

Tools

Collage art requires only the basic tools, and you probably already own many of them. Certain tools will enable you to create with ease—like a metal ruler versus a plastic one (which is not sturdy enough). Look around your house or studio and gather up your tools.

Bristle Brushes

Use these flat- or round-tip brushes to apply matte medium. Select the size of the brush based on the size of the material you need to adhere. You'll want to use a small round-tip brush when applying adhesive to small materials. Use a flat brush when applying adhesive to a larger or broader area.

Synthetic Brushes

I like to use these with acrylic and watercolor paints. They clean easily and are very affordable. It's best to have a variety of tips and sizes, preferably in a range from 0 to 6, with the following tips: round, flat, sashed or angled, and pointer. Take a look at

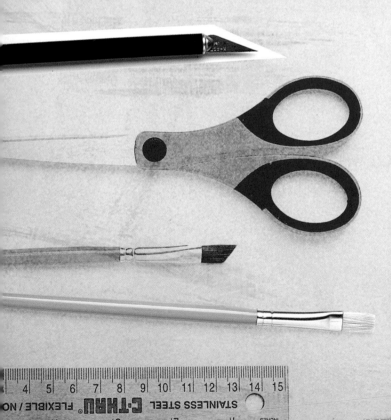

what brushes you already own and see if it is necessary to update.

Scissors

Different types of scissors can achieve different tasks. You will want to have a small pair of scissors, like embroidery scissors, for detailed pieces, and a pair of 6" (15cm) scissors for cutting out shapes. I also have a pair of scissors designated for fabric only. Cuticle scissors are nice to have to cut small detailed circles. Remember, no running with sharp objects!

Craft Knife with No. 11 Blades

A craft knife is perfect for trimming edges and cutting details. I also use my craft knife to help peel backing from different specialty papers.

Cutting Mat

While not essential, a cutting mat saves the wear and tear on any cutting instruments and work surface. The grid on the cutting mat is handy for measuring as well.

Plastic Putty Knives

I use these to flatten and smooth materials once they are affixed to the support. Holding the putty knife at an angle, gently press down while pulling the edge of the putty knife across the material. Excess adhesive will be pushed out by the putty knife, eliminating bubbles and wrinkles. Have a variety of sizes on hand to accommodate your artwork.

2B Pencil

A 2B pencil is my pencil of choice when I am sketching or writing ideas and concepts. Like all artist supplies, pencils are available in an array of choices. The important thing to remember about drawing pencils is the hardness of the lead. The letter "B" represents a pencil with a softer lead, such as 2B, 4B, 6B and so on. The higher the number value, the softer the lead. On the opposite side of the spectrum is the "H" pencil, representing a "hard" lead. In between the "B" and the "H" pencil is the "HB," the middle ground for pencil sets, which is not too hard and not too soft.

Erasers

Rubber-cement pick-up erasers help clean up the excess when using rubber cement. A Pink Pearl or white nylon eraser is a universal eraser for pencil sketch lines and other unwanted marks.

Circle Template

This is a handy dandy-tool for drawing perfect circles.

Proportion Wheel

A proportion wheel is a useful guide to help calculate how to manipulate the size of an original when using a copier. For example, it would help you determine to what percentage you would need to set your copier to enlarge a 4" (10cm) drawing to a 7" (18cm) copy.

Metal Tweezers

Tweezers are great for picking up small items and helping remove the backing from specialty papers.

Sandpaper

Sheets of sandpaper cut into small squares (about 3" × 3" [7.5cm × 7.5cm]) are used to "decollage" art, sand down wood boxes and smooth collage paper's ragged edges. Believe it or not, an emery board can also do a good job of sanding small detailed areas.

Burnisher

A burnisher is used to apply pressure in small areas, smoothing down corners or troubled sections within a collage. This tool resembles a ball-tip pen with an opposing end that has a small, flat edge. You would use a burnisher in areas where a putty knife is too large or cumbersome.

Metal Ruler

Metal rulers are much sturdier than plastic rulers. The hard edge of a metal ruler is recommended when cutting with a craft knife. You may also use a metal ruler as a guide when scoring or tearing paper.

Heavy Machinery

On your playground, you will need a few pieces of heavy equipment. Keep in mind that it is not necessary to purchase these items to complete the projects in this book. We can always find an alternative solution. For example, use a tack hammer and tacks to secure a stretched canvas versus a staple gun or use a press cloth with your iron to keep it clean enough to use on clothes later. No ink jet printer? It's OK; find a copy center and become friends with them. Not into the sewing machine? No sweat; hand stitching works just fine. See, even on a rainy day the playground is in full operation.

- Sewing machine
- Color copy machine or ink jet printer
- Iron, dedicated to art
- Staple gun for stretching canvas

Keeping the Playground Clean

We all know that littering is unacceptable, so think about your work space in the same way. It is OK to have a work in progress. However, even with collage, you will want to keep the area relatively clean and most definitely wash your hands when needed. There's nothing worse than finishing a masterpiece and damaging it by picking it up with dirty hands.

- Water container
- Clean rags
- Palette
- File system to store collage materials

then logarithm of

equi'e next maxi

tions of part (a) o

in t we use

$$y = e^{r+x} \int e$$

nal equation the e

ction, we see that

on of this

BRITISH COLUMBIA

CHAPTER TWO

Collage Elements

Whether you are dabbling in collage for the first time or are an experienced collage artist, this chapter will open new doors. One of the thrills of making collage art is that your sources are unlimited. This chapter will help you create your own original collage materials, which are then readily available for your collage art. By creating your own stash of original Collage Elements, you will no longer struggle with time-consuming searches for just the right background or embellishment. Making decisions on material selection for your collage art will become a simple task.

Mixed-media artists are collectors. Our ideas and concepts are equally as valuable as our materials. We hunt and gather, looking for "just" the right image to collage. Over the years of making collage art, I found I began to take raw materials and alter them. I would weave scraps of paper into shapes, paint book pages, make rub-on transfers from my art and so on. The more Collage Elements I developed, the more I realized I had created my own resource. How refreshing to have materials easily available for your art.

Tip

Organizing your Collage Elements will enable you to create more efficiently. I file my Collage Elements in three-ring binders, using plastic page protectors to sort them. I then label each binder on the spine: Collage Sheets, Flower-Pressed Sheets, Stickers, Rub-On Transfers and so on. This method works well for me; try it or create your own organization system!

JOB 6
RULED TABLE
Plain paper

Collage Sheets

The uses for these collage sheets are limitless. Use a single sheet or combine several for backgrounds; manipulate sizes and make a pattern; cut out designs; stencil; or stamp. Combine vellum paper with other printed images on the copier to produce a layered look on a single sheet, like in *Garden Peace #1* on page 58. This process is used again in *Window Conditioning* on page 92 with a slight variation: the final images are copied on sticker paper. You can indulge your creativity and produce a variety of Collage Sheets ready to use in future projects. See how many variations you can create.

MATERIALS

COLLAGE TOY BOX
scissors

glue stick

COLLAGE RESOURCES
variety of images and papers

OTHER MATERIALS
8½" × 11" (22cm × 28cm) copy paper

color copier

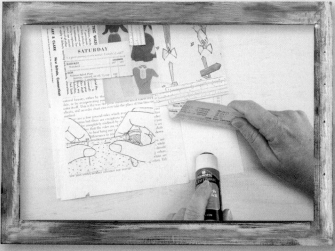

1. Gather images

The fun part of this project is to just randomly pull something from your collage source. Using scissors, trim or cut the image to the desired size.

2. Adhere collage sheet

Use a glue stick to adhere your images to copy paper. Overlap pieces until the entire page is covered. If necessary, trim any overhanging edges to fit the copy paper.

Make ten to fifteen copies of each collage sheet using a color copier. You will want to keep the original intact, making copies on various types of paper, including cover stock, vellum, textured paper and more.

Pattern Collage Sheets

Take advantage of this relatively simple technique to come up with your own unique patterns.

MATERIALS

COLLAGE TOY BOX

scissors

glue stick

COLLAGE RESOURCES

vintage illustrations from children's books

OTHER MATERIALS & SUPPLIES

8½" × 11" (22cm × 28cm) copy paper

color copier

1. Begin repetitive design

Start with a vintage illustration and keep adding more illustrations until you have filled a piece of copy paper. The illustrations may be placed in different directions to help add interest to the composition. Use the glue stick to adhere the images to the paper. As you begin making color copies, set the copier settings to reduce the size of the copy by one-fourth.

Repeat this step with different illustrations until you have made four color copies. Use these copies and continue to repeat the process. Each time you reduce a group of illustrations and make new pages, they start to become a repetitive design or pattern.

2. Make several background sheets

Continue to reduce each full page until you have a page with images so small they make a pattern. When you are satisfied with a completed page, just stop.

Altered Book Pages

The pages of vintage books offer an endless supply of collage sources. By adding a little paint, adding matte medium, cutting out shapes or tracing stencils, you can manipulate each page to be unique. Because this is such a fast process, I suggest creating multiple pages within one sitting. Remember to seek books that are copyright free.

MATERIALS

COLLAGE TOY BOX
acrylic paint set
matte medium
paintbrushes

COLLAGE RESOURCES
vintage book pages

OTHER MATERIALS
palette for paint
cup of clean water

Painted

Use acrylic paint as your surface-enriching medium to create backgrounds for collage work. The transparency of the paint—mixed with matte medium—allows the words from the page to show through.

1. Paint single color

Prepare your work surface for paint. Tear out multiple book pages. Select three complementary acrylic paint colors for your palette. Add a small amount of matte medium to the palette.

Lay out three to four book pages. Begin by dipping your brush into the clean water, followed by one paint color and finally the matte medium. Brush over a large area of your book page. Repeat on other book pages.

2. Layer paint

Lightly clean excess paint off the brush. Dip your brush into a second color and the matte medium. Brush over a small area of the book page, blending the paint into the first color. Repeat on other book pages.

Repeat this step, using a third paint color. Allow the pages to dry.

Tip

You do not have to allow the paint to dry to continue to step 2. In fact, by adding a second color to the wet paint, you blend to make a new color! Try different applications—remember, you have an entire book of pages.

Positive Stencil

A positive stencil will take on the whole shape of the image. Cohesive images work best, but you can add interior details if desired.

MATERIALS

COLLAGE TOY BOX
colored markers
scissors

COLLAGE RESOURCES
vintage book pages
stencil templates

1. Trace image

Tear out multiple book pages. Lay them out on your work surface. Position the stencil template on a book page, looking closely at words or graphics you might want to capture within the shape. Using a fine-tip marker, trace in and around the template.

2. Cut out image

Using scissors, cut the shape out.

Negative Stencil

A negative image creates an empty space perfect for embellishing with markers, pencils and paints. I typically don't cut these images out, but you can if you want to keep track of the pieces.

MATERIALS

COLLAGE TOY BOX
colored markers
colored pencils

COLLAGE RESOURCES
vintage book pages
stencil templates

2. Color in stencil

Using colored pencils, color in the stencil picture as desired.

1. Trace stencil

Tear out multiple book pages. Lay them out on your work surface. Position the stencil on a book page, looking closely at words or graphics you might want to capture within the shape. Using a fine-tip marker, trace in and around the template.

Block Out

Your ruler and a handful of colored markers can transform any book page into a Collage Sheet. This technique requires nothing but imagination. Grab your markers and let's scribble!

MATERIALS

COLLAGE TOY BOX
colored markers
metal ruler

COLLAGE RESOURCES
vintage book pages

1. Choose elements to block out

Using a variety of colored markers, draw lines and shapes over the text of a book page. Create visual interest by varying designs and color. Using the ruler will help add graphic interest. Leave some words and phrases exposed to capture attention.

Organic, Pressed Flowers

Remember those lazy days on the playground when the girls sat in a circle making daisy chains? The sweetness of that memory comes to mind with this next project. A couple years ago, I stumbled on a flower press in an antiques store and immediately began collecting and pressing flowers. It wasn't until recently that I started incorporating them into my art. Consider making several sheets with different flowers in one sitting.

MATERIALS

COLLAGE TOY BOX
glue stick
tweezers

COLLAGE RESOURCES
pressed flowers and leaves

OTHER MATERIALS
wax paper
8½" × 11" (22cm × 28cm) copy paper
color copier

1. Apply glue to paper
Using a glue stick, smear a small dot of glue on the copy paper.

2. Select pressed flower
Pick up a pressed flower with the tweezers and place it on the glue dot.

3. Fill page as desired

Repeat steps 1 and 2 until you've added all the flowers you desire. If the flowers are not adhering properly, lay a piece of wax paper or copy paper over them and gently smooth over the flowers with the heel of your hand.

Using the color copier, make copies of this sheet onto the copy paper. Use the copies in your artwork.

Variations

As you can see in this picture, I selected a purple flower and made a couple variations. After the pages are completed, place on a color copier and make copies from the original sheets. Experiment by copying on sheets of vellum, sticker paper, transparency and rub-on transfer sheets. Protect the original page by placing it into a plastic page protector.

Transparency Art

Printing images on a transparency sheet is a way to create additional layers within your collage art. You may use the transparency as a full sheet or cut out the individual images. Transparency sheets are readily available for most printer types. I like to use the transparency sheets that have adhesive on the back. This makes it easy to adhere the images to the art.

MATERIALS

COLLAGE TOY BOX

scissors

glue stick

transparency adhesive sheets

COLLAGE RESOURCES

vintage illustrations

OTHER MATERIALS

8½" × 11" (22cm × 28cm) copy paper

color copier

1. Select images, adhere and copy

Select images that appeal to you. Cut out the images and glue them to a piece of copy paper. Follow the manufacturer's instructions to make a copy on the transparency sheet.

Vellum Elements

One of the attractions to collage for many artists is the use of texture within the work. Vellum paper has always appealed to me because of its promise of illusion.

MATERIALS

COLLAGE TOY BOX
scissors
glue stick

COLLAGE RESOURCES
vintage illustrations
ephemera
vellum sheets

OTHER MATERIALS
color copier

1. Select images, adhere and copy

Arrange images as desired. Using the copier, copy the image onto a vellum sheet.

Weaving

The simple technique of weaving brings with it a wealth of expressive ideas. The examples in this section will help you bring weaving into your collage art. Here, I'll show you "closed" and "open" weaving, as well as two different ways of adhering the weave together. All these techniques are interchangeable. Practice the following techniques and then take it a step further by creating pieces using different sized strips, materials and patterns.

MATERIALS

COLLAGE TOY BOX

scissors

metal ruler

craft knife

cutting mat

fusible webbing

COLLAGE RESOURCES

vintage book pages

colored paper

OTHER MATERIALS

iron

Closed Weaving

In closed weaving, the vertical strips, or warp, are cut into a single book page. Other strips of paper are woven into the warp strips, but they can't push free of the top and bottom limits of the book page.

1. Prepare book page

Select a page from a vintage book. Starting where the text begins on the page, cut ¼" (6mm) vertical strips (warp). Use the ruler and craft knife to help keep lines straight and accurate.

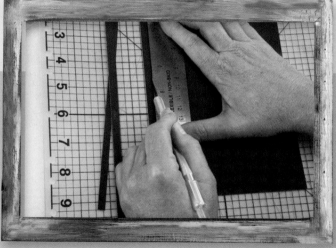

2. Cut strips

To make strips, select papers and cut with a craft knife and ruler on the cutting-mat surface. Repeat this step until you have an adequate amount of paper strips.

Tip

Tissue paper and other lightweight papers make a beautiful contribution to weaving. I have found it is easier to apply the fusible webbing prior to cutting the strips (as described in step 2); this gives the paper stability and enables you to handle the paper without tearing it.

The weight of the fabric or ribbon will dictate whether or not you should apply the fusible webbing before or after cutting and weaving. See how the material handles and weaves. One advantage of using the webbing first is that it stops the fabric from fraying. However, you may choose to have a frayed look. Try a few test strips.

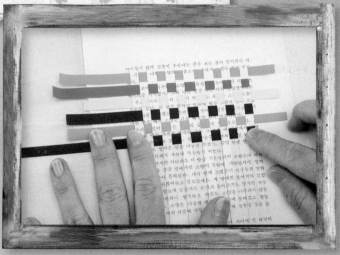

3. Begin weaving weft

Using the basic "under and over" pattern, begin weaving the strips (weft) into the page (warp).

4. Push strips

Periodically push the strips to close gaps so the weave will remain tight.

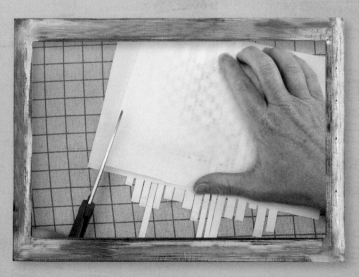

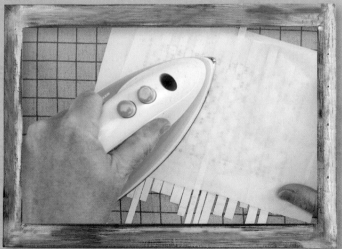

5. Add fusible webbing

Cut a piece of fusible webbing slightly smaller than the weaving.

6. Iron

Following the manufacturer's directions, iron the fusible webbing to the back of the weave. Allow the piece to cool before touching it. Trim the weaving to the desired shape or size.

Open Weaving

The open method of weaving uses loose strips for the warp and the weft, allowing you to select a variety of papers, textiles and other materials.

MATERIALS

COLLAGE TOY BOX

two-sided tape

cutting mat

metal ruler

craft knife

scissors

Double Tack
Mounting Film

COLLAGE RESOURCES

vintage book pages

colored paper

OTHER MATERIALS

8½" × 11" (22cm × 28cm) copy paper

1. Place tape

In open weaving, you will use all strips to weave. Begin by placing a piece of the two-sided tape at the top of the copy paper.

2. Position strips

Use a cutting mat, ruler and craft knife to cut a variety of paper strips ¼" (6mm) wide and at least 6" (15cm) long. Adhere the top of the strips to the two-sided tape. This is your warp.

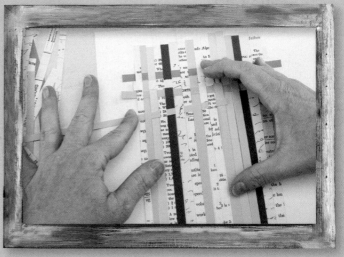

3. Begin weaving

With the remaining strips, begin to weave the weft. To keep the weave tight, periodically push the strips together to close gaps.

4. Add Double Tack Mounting Film

After the weaving is completed, gently fold the weaving back and secure it with a weight, such as a pair of scissors. Cut a piece of Double Tack Mounting Film the size of the weaving. Adhere it to the back of the weaving by peeling off one side of the film and sliding it under the weaving.

5. Secure weaving strips

Secure the weaving to the Double Tack Mounting Film by removing the weight and gently smoothing the weaving down with your hands.

Tip

Live on the edge and try any of these options to achieve your personal look! Cut different sized strips; tear the paper instead of cutting it; integrate fabric strips; or try different patterns of weaving. Try different papers as well and express yourself!

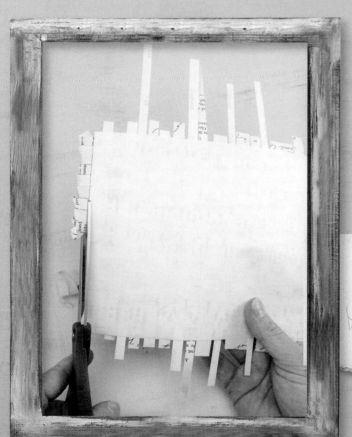

6. Trim edges of weave

Pull the copy paper away from the weaving and trim the edges as shown.

This weave is now ready to be used in a collage.

Tip

I recommend making color copies of your original weaving to have available for different projects. This allows you to create numerous elements from one weaving. It is fun to alter the size of the weaving by enlarging or reducing it on the copier.

Rub-On Transfers

Cruising through the craft store, I discovered a display of different types of paper. The paper products were geared toward scrapbook crafters. But, hey, I like to cross the line, so why not use these products for collage art? Do you have pencil sketches, paintings or photographs? Copy any of these on rub-on transfer sheets and stash them away for future projects.

MATERIALS

COLLAGE TOY BOX

scissors

glue stick

Rub-onz transfer film

craft knife or burnisher

COLLAGE RESOURCES

vintage illustrations

ephemera

OTHER MATERIALS

color copier

8½" × 11" (22cm × 28cm) copy paper

1. Select images, adhere and copy

Select images, cut them out and glue them down onto a piece of copy paper. Following the manufacturer's directions, print the images onto the Rub-onz transfer film. Using scissors, trim closely around an image.

2. Remove transfer backing

As directed by the manufacturer, remove the backing from the rub-on transfer.

Tip

Use the blade of the craft knife to help separate the layers of the transfer film.

3. Burnish

Position the image on your collage. Using a burnisher or the blunt end of the craft knife, gently rub the entire top surface of the transfer image.

4. Remove top paper layer

Using the craft knife, separate the top layer of the Rub-onz transfer film and remove it, revealing the image.

Sticker Paper

Do you have a favorite image? Do you repeat it within your art? Maybe butterflies, flowers or other symbols? Whatever your imagery, sticker elements deliver the goods!

MATERIALS

COLLAGE TOY BOX

scissors or craft knife

two-sided tape or glue stick

sticker paper

COLLAGE RESOURCES

vintage illustrations

ephemera

OTHER MATERIALS

8½" × 11" (22cm × 28cm) copy paper

color copier

Select images, adhere and copy

Select desired images, and then cut and adhere them with two-sided tape or a glue stick onto a piece of copy paper. Follow the manufacturer's directions to copy onto the sticker paper. Trim closely around each image, peel the backing and adhere to your collage art.

Textiles

I love the look and feel of vintage textiles, the time and effort that was involved in handstitching doilies, handkerchiefs and more. Adding these textiles to your collage can sometimes be cumbersome. A solution that works well is to make color copies of the textiles. Another method of adding textiles to collage is to actually print on the fabric. Please note that this is experimental, and you should take special care. If you are unsure of your copier's ability, contact the manufacturer to determine its potential.

MATERIALS

COLLAGE TOY BOX
fusible webbing

COLLAGE RESOURCES
vintage textiles, handkerchiefs or doilies

vellum fabric

OTHER MATERIALS
color copier

8½" × 11" (22cm × 28cm) copy paper, color paper, printable fabric or fabric

iron

1. Copy on different types of paper

Place a doily on the copier bed and make color copies, experimenting with plain paper, vellum and colored paper.

2. Print onto fabric

Try printing on fabric for a refreshing change. Printable fabrics are available through art and craft stores. Follow the manufacturer's instructions to print onto the fabric. Use an iron to adhere fusible webbing to the fabric for support. You can then use the iron to adhere the fabric to the background.

You might be able to print directly onto a piece of fabric you have, but you must check your copier's capabilities before copying onto any unusual materials.

Shape Cut Outs

Many times, I am intrigued by a certain shape or image. I like to see how that particular image or shape would look on different types of paper. For instance, I like to use quilt patterns in my collage art. Along with the variety of papers within one image, I also like to play around with placing it on different backgrounds. You will be amazed at how many different looks you can make with one image. Go out of bounds and give this a try!

MATERIALS

COLLAGE TOY BOX
scissors

your choice of adhesive

COLLAGE RESOURCES
vintage illustration

OTHER MATERIALS
8½" × 11" (22cm × 28cm) copy paper

color copier

Tip

If you chose to use Double Tack Mounting Film as your adhesive, place the film on the back of the patterned paper before you cut out your image.

1. Cut out shape

Find your image and cut it out (If you want to preserve the original image, make a copy and use the copy to make the cut out). Look at how the image is composed. Does it require more than one pattern of paper? Do you want to inset a different pattern or paper for detail in the image? After you have made your decisions, lay the main part of the image onto the paper and cut it out.

2. Cut details

Cut the inset of the image. For example, I have cut out the chest of the bird. Lay the image on the other chosen paper and cut out the inset.

3. Affix to background

Adhere the image to your art using your favorite adhesive. (See the difference in the examples because of the different papers and backgrounds used.)

CHAPTER THREE

Hide-and-Seek

Looking at collage and mixed-media art can sometimes be overwhelming. Images seem to "hide" within the layers of the collage. Trying to isolate the various layers and translate them into techniques can be a daunting task. It may seem impossible for you to figure out, let alone to know where to get started.

The projects in this chapter present the collage process in its simplest form. You will learn to develop collage pieces through basic steps. I use a methodical process of five steps to create a foundation collage. In these projects, you will build up the stash of Collage Elements you created in Chapter Two.

Take a look at *Garden Peace #1* on page 58. The basis of this collage is relatively simple. The background and foreground are from Organic, Pressed Flower Collage Sheets, the middle ground is an Altered Book Page and the finishing touches are a few paper strips and colored-pencil embellishments. This collage project is a prime example of how to break down the process to its simplest form.

petal

pistil

ovary

Other projects, like *Flip Flop #1* on page 38, demonstrate the visual difference of using different backgrounds with the same foreground image. *Clock #1* on page 42 also shows you how the background can influence the feel and look of the collage.

This chapter features vellum, one of my all-time favorite papers. Using vellum in your collage art adds textural qualities along with mystery, making the viewer search through the layers to find the hidden meaning, much like playing "hide-and-seek." I hope you will experiment with vellum and use it in your collage art—seek out its uses in the following pages and enjoy!

MATERIALS

vintage magazine page

5" × 7" (13cm × 18cm) self-adhesive mounting board

colored pencils

shoe image

vellum

color copier

scissors

Double Tack Mounting Film

craft knife

cutting mat

symbol image

matte medium

tweezers

assortment of beads

FLIP FLOP #1

The concept illustrated in this piece shows you how one image can be used with different backgrounds. Because this technique is about layering paper, you will learn how to use different paper for backgrounds with the same image in the foreground. Flip through a vintage magazine or book, find something that catches your eye and use it for the first background selection. If the size is not right, make an enlargement or reduction on a copier. If you want to zoom in on a certain detail, crop it on the copier and make an enlargement. Piece two images together if needed.

1. Adhere vintage magazine page to background

Adhere the vintage magazine page to the self-adhesive mounting board. Smooth it down with your hand.

2. Color image

Using the colored pencils, embellish selected areas as desired.

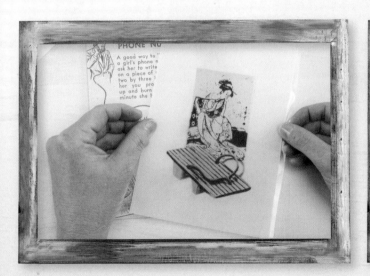

3. Create vellum foreground

Copy the shoe image onto a piece of vellum. Cut the appropriate size of Double Tack Mounting Film and place it on the back of the vellum. Remove the paper backing from the Double Tack Mounting Film and adhere the vellum to the background, smoothing it with the heel of your hand.

4. Trim excess vellum

Turn the artwork facedown. Using the craft knife, trim the excess paper from the edges.

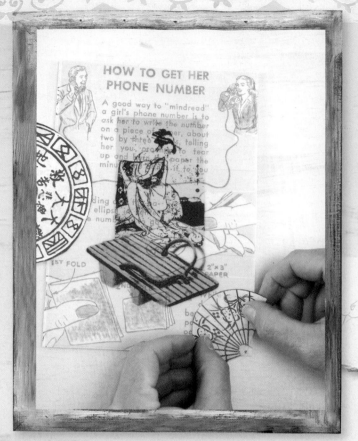

5. Embellish with symbol imagery

Apply Double Tack Mounting Film to the back of the symbol imagery. Cut out the symbols you desire and adhere them onto the vellum.

Tip

You may choose to select cutouts or stickers from your Collage Elements stash. You can use the elements that speak to you to replace images or add further embellishment.

6. Trim embellishments

Turn the artwork face down. Using the craft knife, trim the excess paper from the edges.

7. Add beads

Apply small dots of matte medium where you want to place the beads. Use the tweezers to pick up and position the beads. Allow the matte medium to dry.

Flip Flop #2

You will immediately notice the difference in these two projects. Isn't it amazing how changing a background can influence the feel of art?

This variation features torn pieces of origami paper in the background. I created this piece by tearing the paper into small pieces, adhering them to the self-adhesive mounting board and skipping to step 3.

41

HIGHER ROOTS

If the index of a higher root c̲o̲ ...
other prime facto̲ ... than 2 and
quired ...

CLOCK #1

My friend Becky H. returned from a trip out west with lots of different ephemera, especially watch faces. I made copies of them and stashed them away. When I was working on this project and searching for my foreground image, the watch faces came to mind.

This project is your open door to developing a series of collage art. Continue making this project several times, using different backgrounds, and develop your own collection. By making a copy of the ephemera, it becomes a two-dimensional plane, easily workable in the collage process. If this appeals to you, dig around, find some ephemera, make copies and make art!

MATERIALS

5" × 7" (13cm × 18cm) self-adhesive mounting board

clock image

vellum

color copier

scissors

Double Tack Mounting Film

craft knife

cutting mat

colored markers

vintage book page

COLLAGE ELEMENTS

Weaving page

Vellum Element of a flower

1. Prepare background

Apply the weaving page to the self-adhesive mounting board.

Tip

If your weaving paper is bulky and not flat, consider using a color copy of the weaving instead of the original weaving.

2. Create vellum clock

Copy the clock image onto a piece of vellum. Cut the appropriate size of Double Tack Mounting Film and place it on the back of the vellum. Place the vellum on the background, smoothing it down with the heel of your hand.

3. Add flower cutout

Apply Double Tack Mounting Film to the back of the flower image. Cut out the flower. Position the flower image on top of the vellum.

Tip

At this point you may need to flip the art over and trim any excess edges with your craft knife.

4. Color flower

Use colored markers to embellish the flower.

5. Add vintage book type

Tear part of a page from a vintage book. Apply Double Tack Mounting Film to the back of the page and adhere it to the bottom left side of the art.

If desired, add imagery to the center of the clock.

Clock #2

Like Flip Flop #1 and Flip Flop #2, the visual appearance shifts based solely on background and middle ground choices. See how many different versions of one image you can create. Like making friends on the playground, variety is good!

petal

stamen

pistil

sepal

ovary

stem

MATERIALS

flower image

vellum

color copier

copy paper

scissors

Double Tack Mounting Film

vintage paper, ledger sheet with handwriting

pencil

lace fabric

sticker paper

metal ruler

craft knife

cutting mat

7" × 7" (18cm × 18cm) black paper

sewing machine

ANATOMY OF A FLOWER

I wanted to use a combination of textures to emphasize the beauty of flowers. Looking around, I had a piece of lace, handwritten script and a graphic illustration of a flower. Bingo! Combining these textural elements brought the perfect juxtaposition into a piece of art.

After you have completed this project, continue with other approaches. What different materials can you merge together? Think about opposites: sandpaper and silk, vellum and cardboard. Now think about the subject of the art: Look at images that interest you and colors that excite your senses.

1. Prepare flower template

Make a color copy of the flower image on a vellum sheet. Make a black-and-white copy of the flower image on white copy paper. Using the scissors, cut out the black-and-white flower.

2. Trace flower on handwriting paper

Apply Double Tack Mounting Film to the front of the vintage paper, leaving the backing on the double tack. Lay the cut out flower over the piece of Double Tack Mounting Film. Using the pencil, trace around the flower.

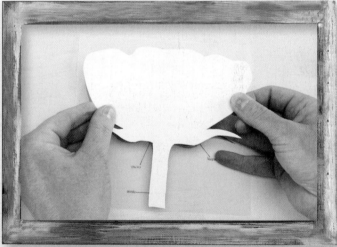

3. Cut out the flower shape

Using the scissors, cut out the flower shape following the pencil outline.

4. Merge vellum

Flip the vellum paper facedown (you should be reading the image backward). Peel the backing off the vintage paper flower shape and adhere to the back of the vellum flower, allowing the words to show through on the front of the flower.

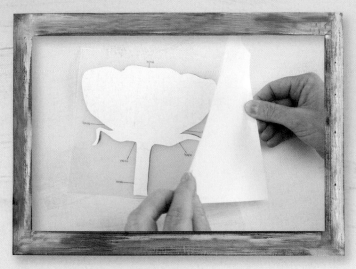

5. Apply Double Tack Mounting Film

Keeping the flower facedown, apply a 6" × 6" (15cm × 15cm) piece of Double Tack Mounting Film to the back.

6. Adhere flower to lace

Make a black-and-white copy of the lace on a sheet of sticker paper. Peel the backing from the flower-vellum piece and adhere to the front side of the lace sticker paper. Using the ruler and craft knife, cut the lace paper to the size of the vellum paper.

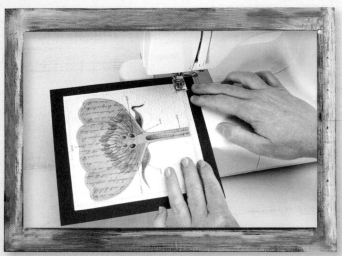

7. Attach image to black background

Peel the backing from the sticker paper. Center the image over the black-paper support and adhere it.

8. Stitch edges

Using the sewing machine, stitch a basic stitch around the outer edges.

Ladybugs Will Rule the World

Never say never. A fellow artist once told me I should "never" use ladybug imagery within my art. Why not? His reply was, "Because the art will 'never' be taken seriously." Well, as you can see, I took this under advisement and decided to create a piece that reflected the strength of this tiny innocent creation. The ladybug is made of Color-aid paper, layered beneath a math line drawing on vellum. The background is composed of math-book pages, sewn together with collage imagery. The doily in the center of the piece adds texture and emphasizes the lines used in the mathematical formulas. So, here's to ladybugs—may they one day rule the world!

(A) 2 ft. ___   (C) 6 ft. ___
(B) 4 ft. ✗   (D) 8 ft. ___

he crew of a boat was increased by ⁷⁄ of its original number. They then had 117 men. How
have originally?

(A)   (C) 91 ✗
       (D) 105 ___

order to reach a building 99 ft.   ed by 32% of its
it?

rain travel is 2½ times as fast   0 miles by bo
0 hrs.?

(A) ___
(B) 25 hrs. ✗   (D) ___

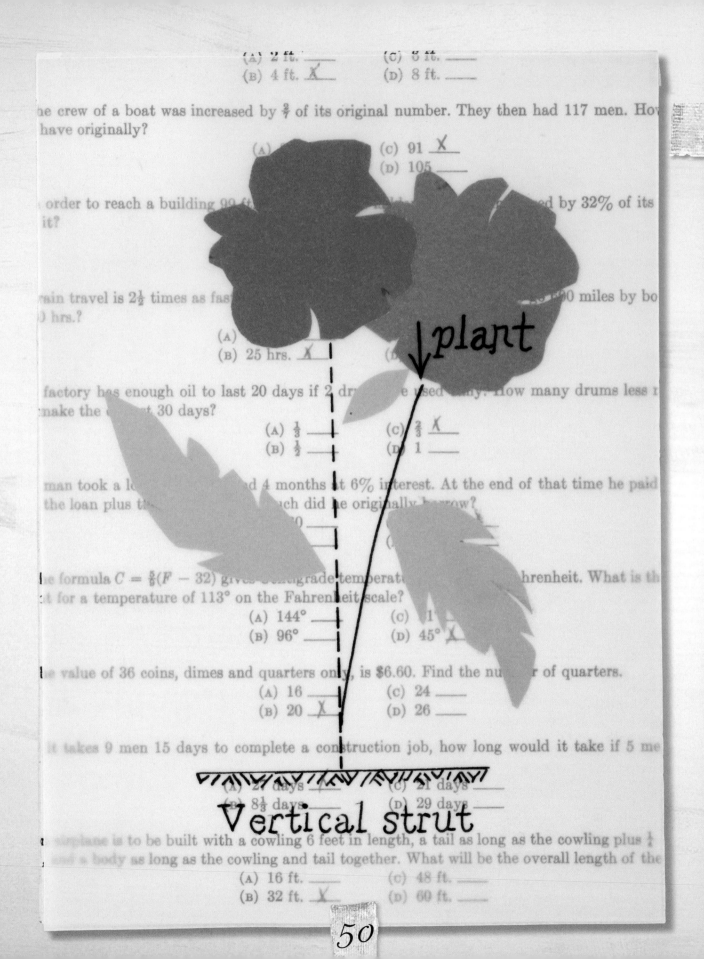

↓plant

factory has enough oil to last 20 days if 2 dr   e used   ny. How many drums less
make the   t 30 days?

(A) ⅓ ___   (C) ⅔ ✗
(B) ½ ___   (D) 1 ___

man took a l   4 months   t 6% interest. At the end of that time he paid
the loan plus t   ch did   e originally   rrow?

          0 ___

he formula $C = \frac{5}{9}(F - 32)$ gives   ntigrade temperat   hrenheit. What is th
t for a temperature of 113° on the Fahrenheit scale?

(A) 144° ___   (C) 1 ___
(B) 96° ___   (D) 45° ✗

he value of 36 coins, dimes and quarters only, is $6.60. Find the nu   r of quarters.

(A) 16 ___   (C) 24 ___
(B) 20 ✗   (D) 26 ___

t takes 9 men 15 days to complete a construction job, how long would it take if 5 me

(A) 2 days ___   (C) 21 days ___
(B) 8⅓ days ___   (D) 29 days ___

Vertical strut

irplane is to be built with a cowling 6 feet in length, a tail as long as the cowling plus ½
a body as long as the cowling and tail together. What will be the overall length of the

(A) 16 ft. ___   (C) 48 ft. ___
(B) 32 ft. ✗   (D) 60 ft. ___

VERTICAL STRUT

One day I sat down with a math book and began flipping through the pages. The formulas and geometrical shapes jumped out at me. Not as math, but as the foundation for flowers, fish, birds and bugs. I traced the linear shapes and adapted them to organic images. Try this project and you will see triangles in a whole new light.

MATERIALS

math formula or geometry shape

color copier

copy paper

proportion wheel

vellum

fine-tip black marker

pencil

vintage book page

5" × 7" (13cm × 18cm) self-adhesive mounting board

craft knife

cutting mat

scissors

Color-aid papers (up to three colors)

embroidery scissors

rubber cement

rubber-cement pick-up eraser

two-sided tape

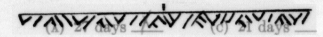

(A) 21 days (c) 21 days

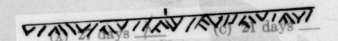

1. Trace image

Start with a geometrical shape from a math book. If needed, copy this image onto a piece of copy paper, reducing
or enlarging the image.

Lay the piece of vellum paper over the image. Using the
fine-tip black marker, trace the image onto the vellum.

2. Sketch flower

Using the vellum drawing as a guide, sketch flowers onto a
piece of copy paper.

3. Adhere book page to background

Decide which side of the book page you want to show
and adhere it to the self-adhesive mounting board. Trim
any excess around the support by flipping over the board
and using the craft knife around the edges.

4. Build flower

Using the scissors, cut the flower shapes out of the copy paper (created in step 2). Trace on the back of the Color-aid paper. Remember this will be a mirror image of the sketch. Using the craft knife or embroidery scissors, cut out the Color-aid paper shapes. Handle the Color-aid paper carefully and try not to bend it.

Using the vellum overlay as a guide, position the flower pieces on the background. Use the rubber cement to adhere the flower pieces to the background. Use a clean piece of copy paper over the flower and press down. Any rubber cement that "leaks" out and around the flower may be removed with a rubber-cement pick-up eraser. Allow the rubber cement to dry.

5. Overlay vellum

Place a piece of two-sided tape at the very top edge of the background. Line up the vellum page with the flower and press down.

Figure 312

This piece evolved because I wanted to utilize magazine scraps backed with Double Tack Mounting Film. I have a box where I toss all the little scraps and pieces from other projects. Take a look at your scrap box and make some art!

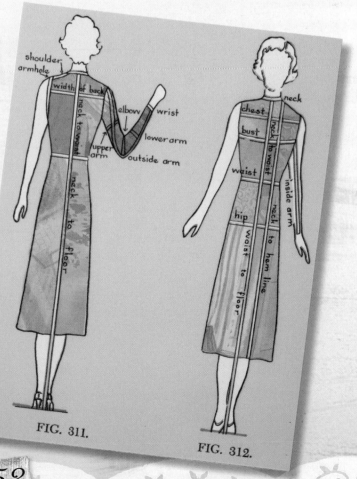

OSCAR, THE NEXT DAY

MATERIALS

scissors

foreign newspaper pages

8" × 10" (20cm × 25cm) self-adhesive mounting board

Double Tack Mounting Film

craft knife

cutting mat

metal ruler

photograph of dog

color copier

copy paper

8½" × 11" (22cm × 28cm) sheet of colored pastel paper

watercolor set

oil pastels

paintbrushes

colored pencils

COLLAGE ELEMENTS

Vellum Element featuring string or thread

Altered Book Page with block out technique

Pets, whether we are pampering them or dressing them in funny costumes, become part of our family. Oscar, the next day, is my "granddog." My youngest daughter adopted him from a shelter a few years ago. He became affectionately known as "Oscar, the next day," when my granddaughter, Aidan, overheard me call him Oscar de la Renta and thought I said, "Oscar, the next day." It's funny how nicknames originate and stay with us.

Do you have a pet? Then I'm sure you have a photograph. That is all you need to get started on this next project.

2. Layer vellum on background

Apply Double Tack Mounting Film on top of the background. Peel the backing paper from the Double Tack Mounting Film and adhere the Vellum Element.

Turn the board facedown. Using the craft knife, trim the excess paper edges.

1. Prepare background

Using the scissors, cut blocks of type from the foreign newspaper and adhere them to the self-adhesive mounting board until it is completely covered.

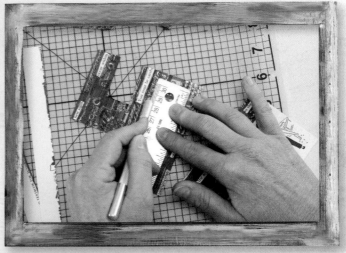

3. Prepare Altered Book Page

Apply Double Tack Mounting Film to the back of the Altered Book Page.

Using the ruler and craft knife, cut small squares and rectangles into the page, sectioning off the words and phrases you want to keep.

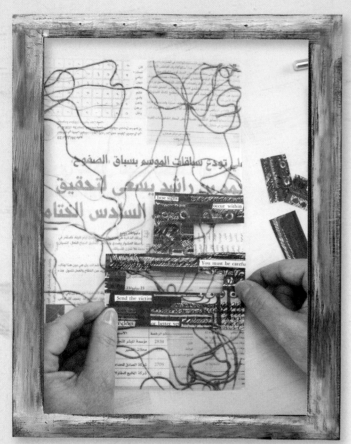

5. Embellish dog image

Make a black-and-white copy of the dog photo, enlarging the image as needed to fill the composition. Using the scissors, cut out the dog image.

On a copier, make a copy of the dog image on a sheet of colored pastel paper. Using the watercolors and oil pastels, embellish the image. Allow the paint to dry.

4. Adhere Altered Book Page to vellum

Peel the backing of the Double Tack Mounting Film and adhere the book page to the vellum.

6. Adhere dog image

Apply Double Tack Mounting Film to the back of the pastel paper image. Using scissors, cut out the dog image.

Peel the backing from the Double Tack Mounting Film and adhere to the background. If desired, use colored pencils to embellish the artwork further.

Oscar, The Day Before

This variation and the original project started with a photo of Oscar, the next day. The background materials include pieces from a newspaper my son-in-law brought to me from Dubai. It was completed using components from my Collage Elements. Of course, I could not resist embellishing Oscar's ears and mouth. I love how changing the colors makes Oscar a little more brooding than the calming effect of the purple and blue tones of the original.

GARDEN PEACE #1

This six-step collage is the quintessential example of how to effectively use your Collage Element resources. The Collage Elements used in this project can vary, resulting in different artwork. I created an entire series, using a variety of pressed flowers and other Collage Elements. Step out of bounds and try a combination of different Collage Elements to create, create, create!

MATERIALS

Double Tack Mounting Film

scissors

12" × 12" (30cm × 30cm) piece of solid color card stock

craft knife

cutting mat

3 strips of colored paper, ¼" × 10¼" (6mm × 26cm) each

circle template

fine-tip black marker

colored pencils in blue and purple

COLLAGE ELEMENTS

Collage Sheet

Organic, Pressed Flowers on vellum sheet

Altered Book Page

59

1. Adhere background to support

Apply Double Tack Mounting Film to the back of the collage sheet.

Using the scissors, trim the collage sheet to 8" × 7¼" (20cm × 18cm). Remove the backing from the Collage Sheet and center it over the card stock. Adhere the Collage Sheet to the card stock.

2. Adhere Altered Book Page

Apply Double Tack Mounting Film to the back of the Altered Book Page. Trim the book page to 5" × 3½" (13cm × 9cm). Adhere the book page to the collage sheet as shown in the photo.

3. Add flower

Select a flower from the Organic, Pressed Flower vellum sheet and apply Double Tack Mounting Film to the selected area. Use the scissors or a craft knife to cut out the flower. Adhere the flower shape to the Altered Book Page as shown.

4. Add paper strips

Apply Double Tack Mounting Film to the backs of the three strips of colored paper. Adhere the strips of colored paper down the right side of the collage as shown.

5. Draw circles

Using the ⅜" (1cm) circle template, draw three circles with the fine-tip black marker along the bottom of the cover stock.

6. Embellish circles

Using the purple colored pencil, fill in the circles. Use the blue colored pencil to add highlights.

Garden Peace #10, from the "Garden Series"

All the formats in the "Garden Series" are on 12" × 12" (30cm × 30cm) supports. In addition to using Collage Elements to create the piece, I used a retro flash card and cut a window opening. Collage Elements make completing a series easy because you always know where you will be starting. The fundamental questions are already answered: What size is the support? What is my concept? What are my material sources?

CHAPTER FOUR

Put on Your Play Clothes

Fiber artists and quilters have been creating tactile collages for decades, piecing textiles and manipulating their qualities, resulting in beautiful works of art and craft. In this chapter, you will see the versatility of textiles when used in traditional collage art.

These projects focus on vintage textiles in particular. A few years ago, I began collecting vintage textiles and started using them in my mixed-media art. My dear friend Becky E. called one day to ask if I wanted some of her mother's things. I was honored because Becky's mother has always held a special place in my heart. When I arrived to collect everything, I was thrilled to receive a box full of vintage textiles. This stash of textiles has been my source for many projects; I can't thank my friend enough for thinking of me. This chapter is dedicated to her and her mother, with love.

The majority of vintage textiles are handmade, offering intricate stitching and designs. Using just part of a vintage textile can enhance the look of your collage art. What should you look for when shopping for vintage textiles? Don't be discouraged by stains or tears within a vintage textile, because very rarely will you use the entire piece.

Vintage ladies' handkerchiefs offer beautiful designs and often tell a story. Vintage doilies have an embroidered design, along with a crotchet trim. Vintage tablecloths are a good resource when you are looking for a large print. The fabric is usually cotton, a perfect candidate for fusible webbing, and you can stretch it over canvas stretcher bars to create a support for your collage!

If you are looking for quantity along with quality, quilting scraps, drapery fabric and bedding are your answer. Quilts that are not quite up to par can offer beautiful textural elements for your mixed-media art.

Vintage clothes are also an untapped resource. The fabrics used in retro clothes are screaming to be part of your art. Men's shirts and ladies' dresses (don't forget the aprons) have textile designs that reflect changes within society.

Whatever the case, look for prints you are attracted to. Remember, you may preserve the vintage textile by making color copies, rather than using the original fabric.

63

MATERIALS

8" × 11" (20cm × 28cm) chipboard

acrylic paint in green and white

paintbrushes

Double Tack Mounting Film

vintage handkerchief

scissors

iron

fusible webbing

COLLAGE ELEMENTS

Shape Cut Out of fleur-de-lis

Altered Book Page

Weaving sheet

.2493

The first thing that attracted me to this vintage handkerchief was its unusual color scheme. The use of earth tones instead of the traditional, feminine pastel colors is quite appealing. I immediately thought of a fleur-de-lis shape that was stashed in my Collage Elements. This shape was cut from an earth-toned recycled paper with math equations copied onto it. I like the way the fabric is slightly transparent when affixed to the painted chipboard. Find yourself an appealing vintage handkerchief, and let's get this party rolling.

1. Prepare elements

Paint the chipboard with the green and white paint, blending it as desired. Allow the paint to dry.

Adhere Double Tack Mounting Film to the back of the vintage handkerchief. Using the scissors, cut the middle section of the handkerchief. Peel the backing from the Double Tack Mounting Film and apply it to the painted chipboard.

2. Build collage

Iron fusible webbing on the Shape Cut Out (fleur-de-lis). Adhere Double Tack Mounting Film to the back of the Altered Book Page and Weaving sheet. Using the scissors, cut several ¼" (6mm) strips from the Weaving sheet.

Adhere each of the Collage Elements to the handkerchief, starting with the Altered Book Page and then the Weaving-sheet strips. Using the iron, adhere the Shape Cut Out to the artwork.

Factors and Roots

Like .2493, this piece uses a vintage handkerchief. The Altered Book Page is printed on vellum, adhered with Double Tack Mounting Film and embellished by using a sewing machine to make zigzag stitching. Once the piece was completed, it was ironed onto chipboard using fusible webbing.

MATERIALS

vintage autograph pages

11" × 14" (28cm × 36cm) self-adhesive mounting board

craft knife

cutting mat

sketchbook paper

fine-tip black marker

iron

fusible webbing

4 or 5 vintage handkerchiefs with flower motifs

scissors

COLLAGE ELEMENTS

Shape Cut Out of bird

Shape Cut Out of a circle

FLOWERS IN A VASE

The "Flower Power" motif has survived many design trends; its longest span in design ranges from the 1920s to well into the 1950s. The ubiquitous floral hand-kerchief lends itself well to becoming a piece of art. The charm of this flower vase recalls the bucolic simplicities of mixed-media art. Creating this project is as peaceful as working in your flower garden—you won't need your garden tools to make this charming piece of art, just a handful of vintage handkerchiefs.

2. Sketch vase

On a piece of sketch paper, using the fine-tip black marker, draw a vase. Turn the paper over and draw over the vase outline. It is important to have the drawing on both sides of the paper.

1. Prepare background

Select vintage papers and affix to the self-adhesive mounting board. Turn over the board, and use the craft knife to trim the edges.

3. Arrange textiles on vase

Iron fusible webbing on the back of all the handkerchiefs. Cut off all four edges of each handkerchief. The strips should be ¼" (6mm) in width and can vary in length. Save the inner portion of the handkerchiefs for step 5.

Pull off the paper backing on the strips so they are ready to iron down. Lay out each strip horizontally, overlapping, until the vase is completely covered.

Iron the fabric strips. Allow the fabric to cool.

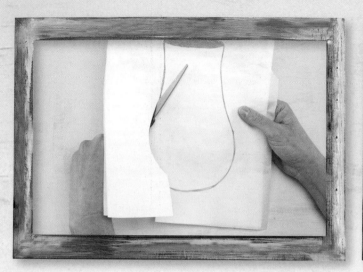

4. Cut out completed vase

Iron fusible webbing onto the back side of the vase shape. Let it cool. Flip the paper over. Using the scissors, cut out the vase shape along the outline.

5. Iron vase and flowers to background

Peel the paper backing from the vase and place it onto the background. Use the iron to adhere the vase shape to the background.

Using the inner portions of the handkerchiefs, cut out the flower images. Arrange the cut out flowers around the top of the vase. As you layer each flower, iron it down until the full flower arrangement is complete.

6. Add embellishments

Look at the composition of the art, and decide whether you want to add anything more. Here, I use a Shape Cut Out of a bird placed on a Shape Cut Out of a circle (both from my Collage Elements).

Use a fine-tip black marker and outline images as desired.

Flower Vase

This larger version of Flowers in a Vase was created using all the same techniques. This gives you an idea of how easily sizes may be shifted using the same concept and themes.

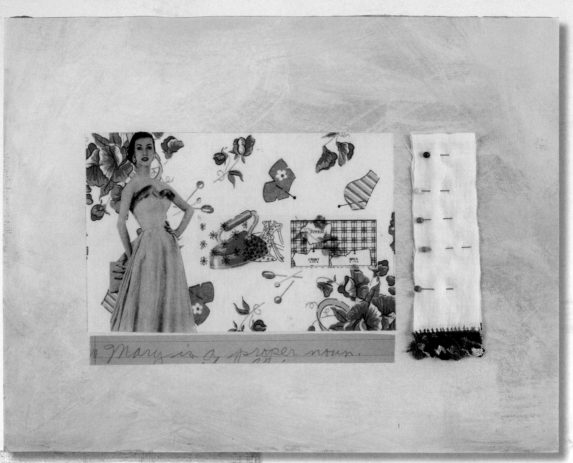

MARY

Finding this handkerchief—with its little domestic items floating along with floral patterns and actual pattern shapes—delighted me to no end. I wanted to combine it with an image of woman from that time period, decked out in formal wear. What a contrast of the times: domestic versus elegant. The straight pins reinforce the idea of domestication. Find a handkerchief that complements or contrasts an image, and create this project for yourself!

MATERIALS

11" × 14" (28cm × 30cm) chipboard

acrylic paint in light blue, light purple and white

palette

paintbrushes

matte medium

vintage handkerchief

iron

fusible webbing

scissors

Double Tack Mounting Film

strip of material 10" × 1" (25cm × 3cm)

5 straight pins with colored heads

COLLAGE ELEMENTS

Sticker Paper image of a retro woman

Sticker Paper image of child's homework paper

Vellum Element featuring an illustration

1. Paint background

Put the light purple, light blue and white paints on the palette. Paint the chipboard with the paint. Add a drop of matte medium to the white paint and paint over the entire background. Paint until you are satisfied with the look. Allow the paint to dry.

2. Adhere textile to support

Select an area of the handkerchief, about 5" × 8" (13cm × 20cm). Following the manufacturer's directions, iron the fusible webbing to the back of the textile. Cut the textile to size and iron it onto the support.

3. Add sticker embellishments

Remove the sticker backing and position the woman on the handkerchief. Repeat with the sticker of the child's homework paper across the bottom of the textile. Adhere Double Tack Mounting Film to the back of the vellum illustration. Remove the paper backing and adhere vellum illustration to the right of the woman.

Cut a strip of material, double the height of the textile in the art (in the example I used a piece of a doily with crotchet trim). Fold the strip of fabric over. Add the straight pins at evenly spaced intervals.

4. Add straight pins to background

Add a narrow strip of the Double Tack Mounting Film to the back of the fabric strip. Remove the paper backing and adhere the fabric strip onto the background.

SCALES AND GRAPHS

When I look at doilies, I feel they are like a sign marquee, stressing a point. The embroidered lines can frame an image or text. The Altered Book Page with the rub-on transfers is framed by the handstitching of the doily. I wanted to play up the contrast of the softness of the doily against the painted acrylic sheet. Do you have an image you want to play up?

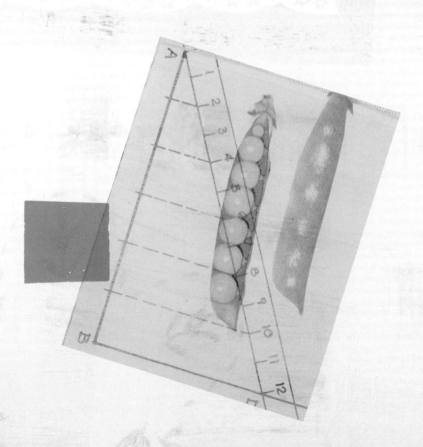

MATERIALS

acrylic paint in yellow and white

palette

paintbrushes

8" × 10" (20cm × 25cm) glazing acrylic sheet

8" × 10" (20cm × 25cm) self-adhesive mounting board

vintage book page of type, large enough to cover the self-adhesive mounting board

craft knife

cutting mat

sandpaper

scissors

vintage doily with handstitching

Double Tack Mounting Film

Color-aid paper in three colors 1" × 1" (3cm × 3cm) square

3 wood squares ½" × ½" (1.25cm × 1.25cm) (you may vary your sizes)

COLLAGE ELEMENTS

Altered Book Page

Rub-On Transfer of fruit or veggie

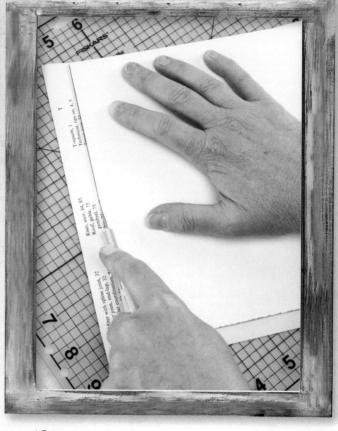

1. Paint glazing acrylic sheet

Pour the paints onto the palette. Paint one side of the glazing acrylic sheet with yellow and white acrylic paint. Allow the paint to dry.

2. Prepare background

Cover the self-adhesive mounting board with the vintage book page. Turn the board facedown. Using a craft knife, trim the excess paper.

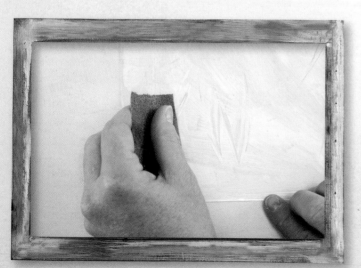

3. Distress glazing acrylic sheet

Using sandpaper, scratch and distress the painted side of the glazing acrylic sheet.

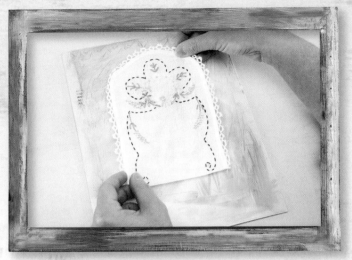

4. Finish background layers

Dust off any dry-paint residue from the glazing acrylic sheet. Add Double Tack Mounting Film to the front side of the background. Peel off the backing and affix the painted side of the glazing acrylic sheet to the background.

If desired, trim the textile to size with the scissors. Apply Double Tack Mounting Film to the back of the textile. Adhere the textile to the front of the glazing acrylic sheet.

5. Layer collage elements

Apply Double Tack Mounting Film to the back of the Altered Book Page and adhere it to the textile.

Add the Rub-On Transfer to the Altered Book Page.

Add the Color-aid paper to the front of the wood squares, adhering with Double Tack Mounting Film. Trim the excess paper as needed. Adhere the wood squares to the art with Double Tack Mounting Film.

Chapter V

The support for this art is constructed using two contrasting textures: a piece of burlap and a vintage handkerchief. I pulled an Altered Book Page and sticker images of a woman and the planet Earth from my Collage Elements stash. The art is further embellished with paper strips and a graphite pencil. Notice how the spherical shape of the flower pattern on the handkerchief mimics the image of the Earth, and the subtle shade of orange in the earth image complements the color of the flower pattern. Try looking for collage elements that will enhance other areas of your artwork.

TOMORROW

76

This is a great example of stretching vintage textiles on canvas stretcher bars. In this project, I use a piece of vintage fabric as my support, adding other collage components before stretching it onto the canvas stretcher bars. Look at your vintage textiles. Do you have fabric that can be a support for your mixed-media projects?

MATERIALS

acrylic paint in rose, crimson, green and white

palette

matte medium

paintbrushes

18" × 18" (46cm × 46cm) green fabric

iron

fusible webbing

11" × 11" (28cm × 28cm) vintage handkerchief

text of the word "tomorrow"

one sheet of vellum

Double Tack Mounting Film

color copier

image of a woman

1 sheet of pastel colored paper

proportion wheel

scissors

4 14" (36cm) stretcher bars

staple gun

COLLAGE ELEMENTS

Altered Book Page

Vellum Element featuring a graphic illustration of a sewing technique

1. Paint background fabric

Pour the acrylic paints onto the palette. Dilute the acrylic paint with matte medium; one dot of medium to four dots of paint. Look at your fabric background and embellish areas with acrylic paint. Brush the paint on the fabric with a small flat brush. After you have achieved the desired effect, allow the paint to dry.

2. Layer items with fusible webbing

Following the manufacturer's directions, iron fusible webbing to the textile and Altered Book Page. Iron the handkerchief in the center of the painted background. Allow it to cool.

Layer the book page in the center of the handkerchief and adhere it with the hot iron. Allow it to cool before continuing.

3. Add embellishments

Select embellishments from your Collage Elements stash, such as text and Vellum Element of graphic illustrations. Adhere these elements to the textile using the Double Tack Mounting Film.

4. Fuse woman to textile

Copy the image of the woman onto the pastel colored paper and enlarge or reduce the size of the image if desired. Following the manufacturer's directions, iron fusible webbing to the image of the woman. Using the scissors, cut the image out. Fuse the woman to the Altered Book Page with the iron.

If desired, add more Collage Elements.

6. Stretch art onto frame

On a clean surface, lay the art facedown. Place the stretch frame on top of the fabric. Fold the edge of the fabric over and then pull the fabric tight and staple to the frame. Repeat on the opposite side.

5. Assemble stretcher bars

Connect the stretcher bars to form a frame.

7. Fold corners

After you have the two opposing sides stretched and stapled, fold the corners and staple; this process is similar to folding the edges on boxes or gifts. The objective is to have a tightly pulled corner, without bulky fabric. It may be necessary to use scissors and cut away some of the excess fabric.

Always

When you find a background you like, don't hesitate to continue using it to produce other art. Having a common denominator is a great way to jump-start a series. In this piece, I painted the flowers in the same color scheme; however, you may choose to use other colors for a different look.

Add and Subtract

So much of collage work depends on what you add or take away while you're creating. Highlighting something in the background, tearing a piece of paper just so, using an image again and again—all these choices can make or break a piece or, at the very least, dictate how you feel about it.

In this chapter, we'll work on adding and taking away to bring out the playful art inside you! I'll introduce you to "found poetry," the art of combining fragments of text to create a poem. The combination of this writing technique and collage is a marriage made in heaven, like doughnuts and coffee, peanut butter and jelly. Found poetry is enjoyable; try it and see what you come up with!

Repeating images is another fun concept. This isn't an exercise in memorization; it's a chance to create with a favored image or images. Will the individuality of the image get lost within the repetition, or does the repetition claim a new identity? You decide—and while you're at it, have fun and make some art!

Interactive illustrations are commonly found in "pop-up" books, enticing readers to pull the tab, turn a wheel or open a door. I love the fact that art can also be interactive. Challenge yourself to come up with

or more!

THE
URE
YOU
ANT.

Charting your Independence

with

No Limit

5

other interactive forms in your art: how about a zipper, pocket sleeve, buckle or spinning wheel?

While collage can offer an almost limitless range of ingredients to provide the formal elements of design fundamentals, decollage does the same in reverse. Instead of building up layers to create art, decollage works back to front. Have you ever noticed a lacerated billboard where the advertisement is long gone, with the beautiful paper remnants showing? You will be intrigued by this technique of layering, building and deconstructing.

We'll use the techniques you've already learned to make specialized Collage Elements for your works of art. You'll see you can create Collage Elements when the mood strikes. Join me in these fun games—you can count on some great art!

MATERIALS

Double Tack
Mounting Film

14½" × 20" (37cm × 51cm)
foamcore

pencil

sketch of abstracted figure

color copier

copy paper

scissors

Color-aid papers (up to
three colors)

embroidery scissors

craft knife

cutting mat

two-sided tape

rubber cement

rubber-cement
pick-up eraser

fine-tip black marker

COLLAGE ELEMENTS

2 Pattern Collage
Sheets, 8½" × 11"
(22cm × 28cm) each

ORIGINAL CAST

The abstract form in the foreground is a perfect balance to
the multiple details of this repetitive-design background.
Take a close look at the background and notice how each
square is its own illustration. What if you use only one repeated image: Does it lose its identity and gain a new one? Play
around with different images and ideas and see what you
come up with for your repetitive design!

1. Apply background sheets to support

Apply Double Tack Mounting Film to the back of both pattern collage sheets. Peel away the backing paper from the Double Tack Mounting Film and adhere the sheets to the foamcore.

2. Create color insets

Sketch an abstract figure or shape. Make several copies of the sketch to be used as templates. Cut out the templates, labeling the parts. Trace each template to the front of a piece of Color-aid paper. Using embroidery scissors or a craft knife, cut out the pieces.

To make the color inset, use the craft knife to cut window openings (in this example, it is the circles). Cut square pieces of Color-aid paper in a variety of colors large enough to fill in the openings. Adhere the pieces with two-sided tape, placing the front side of the squares to the back side of the circles.

3. Add figure

Gently brush the back side of the Color-aid paper with rubber cement and press it lightly onto the background. Continue to assemble the figure and composition on the background. Remember to use the rubber-cement pickup eraser to eliminate any leakage around the image. It is best to wait for the rubber cement to dry (about ten to fifteen minutes) before erasing.

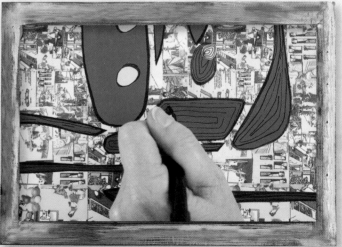

4. Outline and embellish

After the rubber cement is dry and the images are secure, use a black fine-tip marker to outline the figure and add line embellishments throughout the composition as desired.

OPEN DOOR POLICY

This beautiful image of a young woman sitting peacefully in a meditative state prompted the collage. I found that it defined women, provoked calmness and relayed our inner beauty. This is a sweet piece of art that invites the viewer to look beyond the expected. Find an image that speaks to you, and see what doors (or windows) it can open.

MATERIALS

acrylic paint in blue, green, yellow and white

palette

paintbrushes

16" × 20" (41cm × 51cm) gallery wrapped canvas

landscaping and tree images

color copier

copy paper

embroidery scissors

matte medium

putty knife

tissue paper from sewing pattern

craft knife

cutting mat

door image

3–4 sheets of manila drawing paper

proportion wheel

Double Tack Mounting Film

metal ruler

page of text (for inside door)

colored pencils

2 sheets of Color-aid paper

printer

Kodak Premium Photo paper, compatible with your printer

scissors

image of woman

two-sided tape

fine-tip black marker

small black button

1. Prepare background

Pour the acrylic paint onto the palette. Paint the canvas using a mixture of brilliant blue and white. Allow the paint to dry.

Make color copies of the trees and landscape on white copy paper. Using the embroidery scissors, trim the images carefully to get the sections you want. Apply matte medium with a clean paintbrush to the background and adhere the paper to the canvas. Smooth down the paper with a putty knife.

2. Blend background with paint

Look at the composition and add paint to the leaves and grass to help blend the paper at the seams of the separate images. Allow the paint to dry thoroughly.

3. Apply pattern tissue paper to background

Brush the entire canvas and edges with a light coat of matte medium and cover the background with the tissue paper. Smooth it down with the heel of your hand, allowing wrinkles and folds for texture.

4. Trim excess paper

After the matte medium dries, turn the canvas over. Using the craft knife, trim any excess paper.

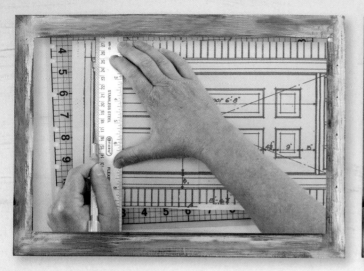

5. Assemble door

Make a black-and-white copy of the door on the manila drawing paper. Reduce or enlarge the image as needed; if you want a large door, you can print the image in two halves, but you will need to piece together the top and bottom copy of the door. The door shown is 15" × 7½" (38cm × 19cm).

Apply Double Tack Mounting Film to the back of the door. Using a ruler and craft knife, trim around three sides of the actual door. Score the side of the door where the hinges would be so you can open and close the door (do not cut through the backing).

6. Trim backing paper from inside of door

Turn the door ensemble over, facedown. Using the ruler and craft knife, cut the backing paper from the Double Tack Mounting Film. Apply just enough pressure to cut through the backing paper; be careful not to cut the paper of the door.

7. Add text sheet to inside of door

Measure the size of the door. Make a black-and-white copy of the text (for the inside of the door) on the manila drawing paper. If the image needs to be larger, enlarge it on a copier. Cut the text copy to fit the measurement of the door.

Peel the Double Tack Mounting Film from the back of the door. Adhere the text to the back of the door.

8. Embellish door

Using colored pencils, color the front door as desired.

9. Assemble woman and Color-aid paper

Decide which of the Color-aid paper colors will go at the top and bottom of the image. Cut the Color-aid papers as desired, as long as they fit the dimension of the inside of the door with an extra ½" (1.25cm) on all sides. Lap the edges of the Color-aid over each other, securing them with a piece of two-sided tape. Back the two pieces of Color-aid paper with Double Tack Mounting Film.

Print a black-and-white copy of the woman onto the photo paper. Apply Double Tack Mounting Film on the back of the woman. Using the embroidery scissors, cut out the image. Peel the backing from the Double Tack Mounting Film and adhere the woman to the front side of the Color-aid paper.

10. Position image under door frame

Turn the door ensemble over. Pick up the Color-aid paper ensemble and place it facedown on the back of the door ensemble. Trace the outer edges of the Color-aid ensemble using a black marker.

12. Remove backing paper

Gently peel the backing paper from the cut lines.

11. Trim backing paper

Using the ruler and craft knife, trim the backing paper of the Double Tack Mounting Film on the lines you drew in step 10. Apply only enough pressure to cut through the paper backing, being careful not to cut the door.

13. Adhere Color-aid inset

Position the Color-aid paper ensemble facedown over the exposed Double Tack Mounting Film and adhere it.

14. Embellish with black marker

Turn the door ensemble over. It should open to reveal the Color-aid paper and the woman. Now that the door and door inset are complete, peel the backing of the Double Tack Mounting Film from the door and adhere to the canvas. Press it down with the heel of your hand.

Use a dot of matte medium on the door and adhere the black button for the door knob. Allow the matte medium to dry.

Using the black fine-tip marker, draw lines and circles to unify the composition and enhance lines.

**Open Door Policy
with the door closed**

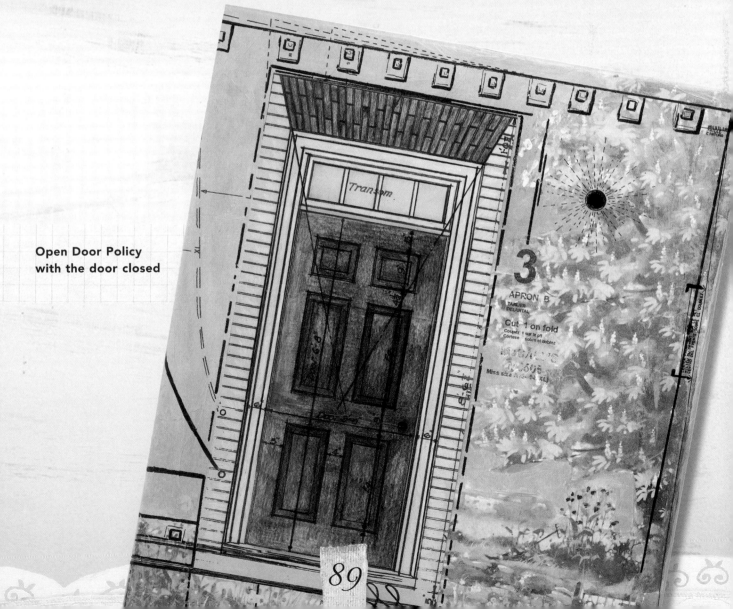

THE FUTURE YOU WANT

When working on art, I sometimes listen to audible books. The words become images in my head, and the images progress to works of art. After reading *Mornings Like This: Found Poetry* by Annie Dillard, I decided to combine the art technique of "cut-up" with the idea of found poetry. This project was so enjoyable because it could move in any direction with a serious voice or a lighthearted one.

MATERIALS

vintage magazine pages

scissors

11" × 14" (28cm × 36cm) self-adhesive mounting board

your choice of imagery and illustrations

Color-aid paper

craft knife

cutting mat

fine-tip black marker

Tip

The cut-up technique has long been one of my favorites. The basic idea is to take a page of text, cut it in pieces with words on each piece and then rearrange the page pieces into a new text.

For *The Future You Want*, I cut out headlines, subtitles and phrases from different magazines and then rearranged them into a poem. Explore your resources: cut-up and combine e-mails, song lyrics or movie titles.

Another method to make found poetry is to cut the page into quarters, rearrange them and then rewrite the prose, adding words to compensate for the word breaks.

1. Select text

Flip through vintage magazines and look for headlines, phrases and images that appeal to you. Cut them out.

Peel off the backing paper on the mounting board and adhere the collage pieces, starting with the text. Stagger them unconventionally to add interest to your art.

Tip

Self-adhesive mounting board is wonderful, but do remember that images cannot be removed or repositioned after you stick them on—plan carefully!

2. Add images and color

Begin to add color and images throughout your poem. It may be necessary to cut some of the images into different shapes or sizes. Play around with the composition and balance. I recommend using the Color-aid paper last to complete areas that demand specific sizes; trim the paper as needed to fill in the empty spaces.

3. Trim edges

Flip the board over. Using the craft knife, trim the excess paper from all the edges.

4. Embellish artwork

Use the fine-tip black marker to draw lines, unify the piece and add embellishments.

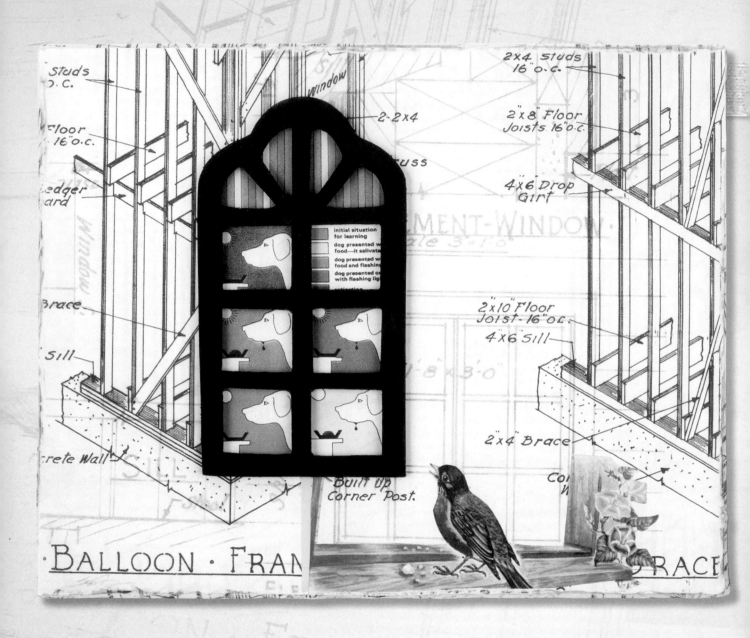

WINDOW CONDITIONING

The complex background of this project is deceiving—it is actually one image copied onto itself. This is an example of how to repeat one image to create a new look. By copying the image on tracing paper, layering it over the original image and making a new copy, the images fade into one another. You can try this method using different types of papers to achieve different looks. Consider using transparent sheets or colored vellum; try manipulating the size of the image on one copy. There are lots of possibilities for your collages.

This project offers an excellent opportunity to create new items for your Collage Elements stash. For example, in step 1, you will be making collage sheets for the background; go ahead and produce several different images to stash away for future projects. In step 4, you are asked to copy a bird image onto sticker paper—take this opportunity to complete a variety of images (along with the bird) on a full sheet of sticker paper. You'll come away from this project with a piece of art and a handful of new Collage Elements!

MATERIALS

2 architectural drawings

color copier

3–4 sheets of 8½" × 11" (22cm × 28cm) 25-lb. tracing paper

3 sheets of 8½" × 11" (22cm × 28cm) sticker paper

metal ruler

8" × 10" (20cm × 25cm) gallery wrapped canvas

matte medium

burnisher

sandpaper

craft wood window

acrylic paint in black

paintbrushes

pencil

copy paper

6 different dog images

scissors

stripe design for arch of window

glue stick

bird image

1. Prepare background

Copy one page of the architectural drawing onto the tracing paper. Use the tracing-paper copy to overlay onto the other architectural drawing and make two more copies on tracing paper and one copy on the sticker paper.

Measure and cut the tracing-paper copies to fit around the four edges of the canvas. Adhere to the canvas using matte medium. Your canvas should be blank in the center and have tracing paper along the perimeter and sides. Allow the canvas to dry thoroughly.

2. Add sticker paper

Cut the sticker paper to 8" × 10" (20cm × 25cm). Position and adhere the sticker paper to the front of the canvas. Burnish the edges of the sticker paper to blend them into the tracing paper on the canvas. If needed, use sandpaper to help bend all the paper's edges.

3. Create window template

Sand the wood window frame. Using the black paint, paint the window frame. Allow the paint to dry thoroughly.

Using the window as a guide, draw a template onto a piece of plain copy paper. Cut the dog images to fit into the window insets of the template. Do the same for the striped design paper in the arch of the window. Glue the images and paper down with the glue stick. Make a color copy on a sheet of sticker paper.

4. Add bird

Make a color copy of the bird image on sticker paper. Using the scissors, cut out the image. Play around with the placement of the window and bird. The bird image must be adhered to the background before the window. When you are satisfied with the position of the bird, remove the sticker-paper backing and affix it to the canvas.

5. Adhere window

Using the scissors, cut out the window-inset image and adhere it to the back of the window, faceup, using the glue stick. Peel off the sticker-paper backing and position the window onto the canvas.

Detail of Window Conditioning

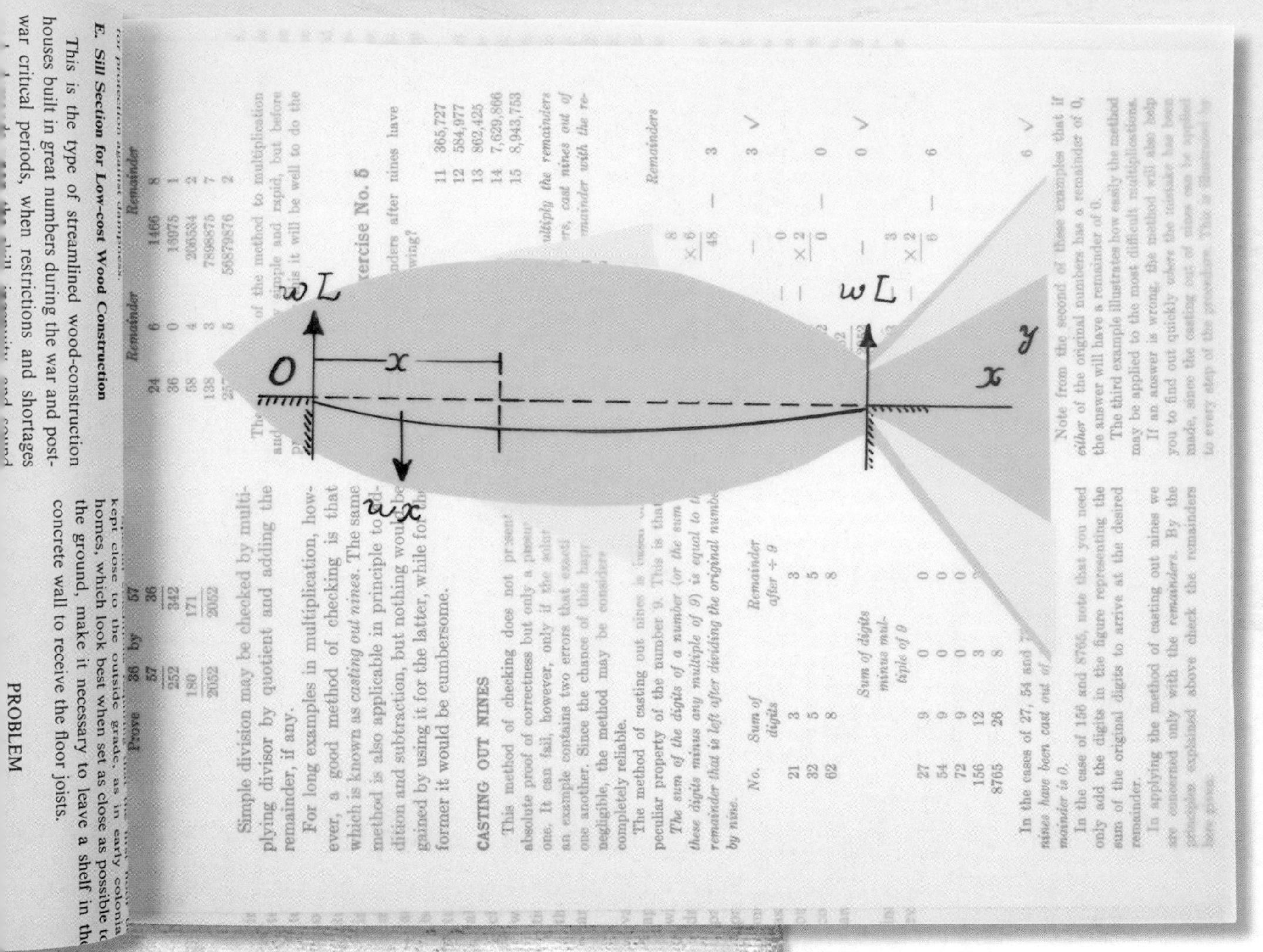

Simple division may be checked by multiplying divisor by quotient and adding the remainder, if any.

For long examples in multiplication, however, a good method of checking is that which is known as *casting out nines*. The same method is also applicable in principle to addition and subtraction, but nothing would be gained by using it for the latter, while for the former it would be cumbersome.

CASTING OUT NINES

This method of checking does not present absolute proof of correctness but only a *proof* one. It can fail, however, only if the solution an example contains two errors that exactly one another. Since the chance of this happening negligible, the method may be considered completely reliable.

The method of casting out nines is based peculiar property of the number 9. This is that *The sum of the digits of a number (or the sum these digits minus any multiple of 9) is equal to remainder that is left after dividing the original number by nine.*

No.	Sum of digits	Remainder after ÷ 9
21	3	3
32	5	5
62	8	8

		Sum of digits minus multiple of 9
27	9	0
54	9	0
72	9	0
156	12	3
8765	26	8

In the cases of 27, 54 and 72 the *nines have been cast out of* **mainder is 0.**

Remainder

24	6	1466	8
36	0	19075	1
58	4	206534	2
138	3	7866675	7
255	5	56879676	2

Exercise No. 5

11	365,727	
12	584,977	
13	862,425	
14	7,629,866	
15	8,943,753	

Remainders after nines have ... following?

... multiply the remainders ... ers, cast nines out of ... mainder with the re-

Remainders

8			>
× 6			3
48	3		3 ✓

	0		>
	× 2		0
	0		0 ✓

	3		>
	× 2		6
	6		6 ✓

Note from the second of these examples that if either of the original numbers has a remainder of 0, the answer will have a remainder of 0.

The third example illustrates how easily the method may be applied to the most difficult multiplication.

If an answer is wrong, the method will also help you to find out quickly where the mistake has been made, since the casting out of nines can be applied to every step of the procedure. This is illustrated by *...*

In the case of 156 and 8765, note that you need only add the digits in the figure representing the sum of the original digits to arrive at the desired remainder.

In applying the method of casting out nines we are concerned only with the *remainders*. By the principle explained above check the remainders *...*

MATH MADE SIMPLE, INFINITE FISH

Mathematicians use graphic diagrams to illustrate their formulas, and, in doing so, they also create art. The meticulous line drawings, sweeping curves and symbols are all quite lovely, waiting for you to add your own creative touch. That is exactly what I have done in this piece. I started with a math formula and used it as the jumping-off point to complete a drawing. Create a whole series—even add a cover—and stitch it all together for your own special book. Go grab your math book, and let's do some homework!

MATERIALS

geometry diagram

color copier

copy paper

pencil

fine-tip black marker

60-lb. vellum 8" × 10" (20cm × 25cm)

scissors

Color-aid paper, 2 colors

rubber cement

page from math book

rubber-cement pick-up eraser

two-sided tape

decorative rice paper (optional)

sewing machine

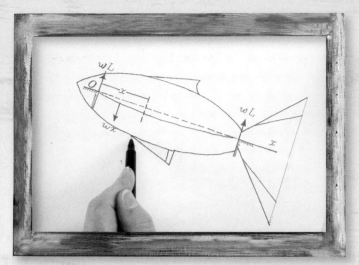

1. Create sketch from math equation

Using a copy machine, enlarge a geometry diagram on regular copy paper. From this diagram, sketch something that follows the shape of the equation. This particular equation reminded me of a fish.

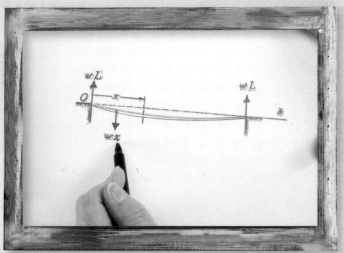

2. Trace geometry diagram on vellum

Using a fine-tip black marker, trace the copy of the geometry diagram onto the vellum paper.

3. Create fish shape from Color-aid paper

Using the scissors, cut out the fish created in step one. Using this image as a template, create a Shape Cut Out (see page 35) on the Color-aid paper.

Brush a light coat of rubber cement on the back of the fish and adhere it to the math book page. Allow the rubber cement to dry. Clean up any rubber-cement residue with the rubber-cement pick-up eraser.

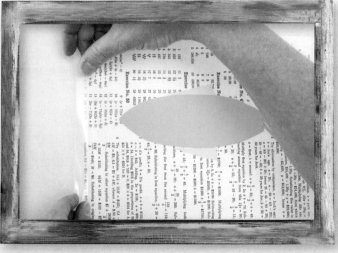

4. Add tape

Adhere a piece of two-sided tape down the left side of the book page.

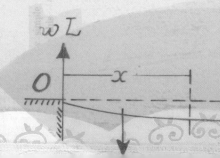

6. Sew booklet

Assemble the pages and book cover so all the pages line up. Using the sewing machine, secure the book pages with a zigzag stitch.

5. Add vellum overlay and create remaining pages

Carefully layer the vellum sheet with the equation over the fish; line it up to match the design of the fish.

To make a booklet, create several more pages by repeating steps 1–5 using different equations for each page of the booklet. If desired, make a cover. In the example, I printed on a sheet of decorative rice paper.

After you have the desired number of pages, continue to step 6.

7. Trim pages to size

Using the scissors, trim the pages to size.

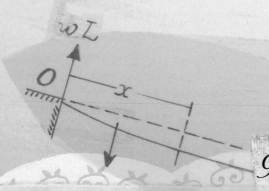

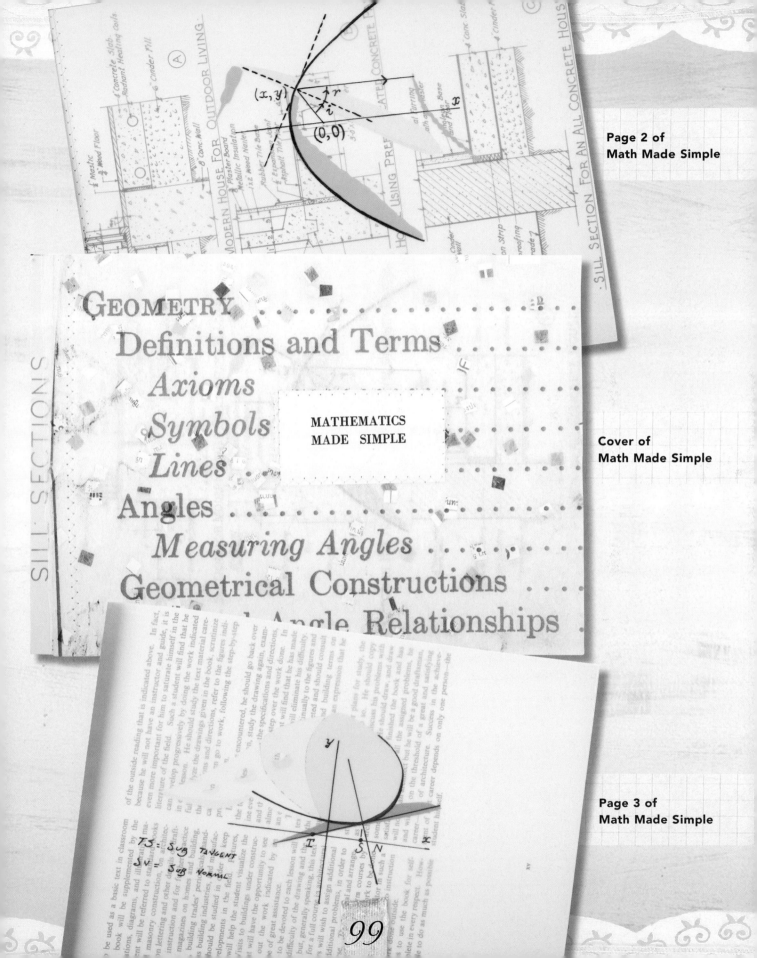

Cover of Math Made Simple

GRASSHOPPERS

Once again, math is the main element for developing this project. The grasshoppers you see in the foreground are drawn using a math formula as the starting point. Can you see the shapes in the grasshoppers' bodies?

The background is developed using the decollage technique: applying layers of paper and then removing layers from selected areas. Decollage can create unexpected results with each layer.

MATERIALS

matte medium

putty knife

16" × 16" (41cm × 41cm) chipboard support

vintage handwritten papers

scissors

vintage magazine pages

paintbrushes

sandpaper

geometry formulas

pencil

sketch paper

fine-tip black marker

1. Prepare background

Using the matte medium and putty knife, cover the chipboard with the vintage handwritten pages, overlapping them. Allow the matte medium to dry.

2. Add magazine branches

Using the scissors, cut the magazine pages into various branch shapes and sizes. Use a paintbrush and matte medium to adhere them to the background. If needed, use the putty knife to smooth the papers as you apply them. Allow the matte medium to dry.

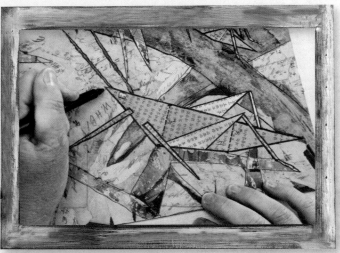

3. Decollage artwork

Using the sandpaper, gently sand the branches and background. As you sand the branches, you'll notice the background may show through; this is decollage. Continue to sand until you have the desired textured look.

With a clean, dry brush, sweep over the piece to remove any dust or grit residue.

4. Add grasshoppers

Using geometry formulas, sketch a grasshopper. Make the shape of your grasshopper linear. Use these sketches as a template to make Shape Cut Outs (see page 35) on the Altered Book Pages. Use separate pages for the body, legs and antennae.

Using matte medium, add and assemble the grasshoppers on the background as desired. Allow the matte medium to dry completely. Outline with the black fine-tip marker to give the grasshoppers definition.

FRESH ORANGES

Yummy—there's nothing better than a slice of a ripe, juicy orange. My mouth waters just thinking about it. In *Fresh Oranges*, you will have the opportunity to create a scene. Project more interest by using images that are off scale, like the large oranges on the small table. Let the decollage technique work its magic as a textural background. Add dimensional objects within the composition to help balance it. Are you ready for some vitamin C?

MATERIALS

palette

acrylic paint in yellow, blue, black-and-white

paintbrushes

11" × 14" (28cm × 36cm) gallery wrapped canvas

vintage magazine pages

vintage book pages

matte medium

putty knife

sandpaper

wood window

pencil

glue stick

fine-tip markers in red and black

metal ruler

colored pencils

COLLAGE ELEMENTS

Sticker Paper with images of an orange, table, cat on a rug, figure in a chair, freestanding chair and bird

1. Paint background

Pour the acrylic paints onto the palette. Using the paint-brush, paint the canvas yellow and white, blending the colors as desired. Allow the paint to dry.

2. Adhere paper to background

Tear and cut the vintage magazine and book pages into pieces of varying shapes and sizes. Using the matte medium, adhere the torn paper pieces, overlapping the papers in some places.

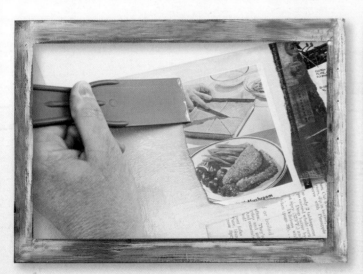

3. Smooth paper pieces

When you use a variety of papers, the texture and thickness can vary. Smooth the paper using the putty knife as you collage the paper onto the canvas.

When you are satisfied with the coverage of the background, allow the matte medium to dry.

4. Decollage background

Using the sandpaper, sand away the background pages to allow images to "peep" through. When you are satisfied with the texture, use a clean, dry brush to remove any dust or grit from the canvas.

5. Apply collage images

Look at the canvas and determine how you want your composition, or scene, to look. Try to achieve balance and unity by carefully placing the images that complement one another. Remember to work back to front; for example, put the table down before adding the oranges.

Apply the Collage Element pieces as desired.

6. Add window detail

Place the craft wood window on the canvas in its designated spot (do not adhere it at this time). Using the pencil, trace an outline of the window and its openings.

Remove the window. Using the paintbrush, paint inside the window the outline with a mixture of light blue paint and matte medium. Allow the paint to dry.

7. Adhere window to art

Using the sandpaper, smooth the craft wood window. Paint the window black and allow it to dry.

Using the glue stick, adhere the window to the background over the painted area.

8. Embellish artwork

With the black marker, draw fringe around the rug; with the red marker, trace the lines on the table. Create unity within the composition by connecting imagery using a black marker to draw lines; use the ruler to create a clean, graphic look. Highlight areas using a white pencil; deepen colors using the colored pencils.

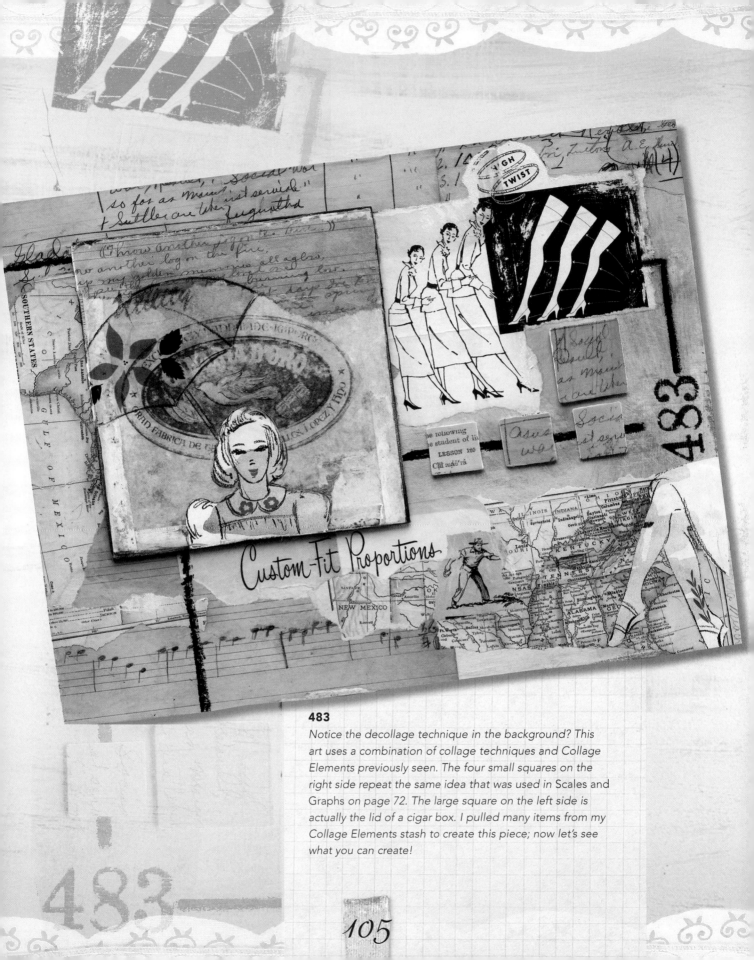

483

Notice the decollage technique in the background? This art uses a combination of collage techniques and Collage Elements previously seen. The four small squares on the right side repeat the same idea that was used in Scales and Graphs on page 72. The large square on the left side is actually the lid of a cigar box. I pulled many items from my Collage Elements stash to create this piece; now let's see what you can create!

CHAPTER SIX

Stand Out on the Playground

This chapter is all about standing out! Get your artwork noticed by using different forms of dimension. These techniques bring focus to the foreground of the collage by moving it forward, literally.

Pop-up images are usually comprised of only one to two pieces; they are basically Shape Cut Outs taking center stage. I love to use foam pop-ups, which can be found in a variety of sizes, shapes and widths, making them ideal to work with in collage. Think about using pop-ups in different depths, layering and stacking images.

Shape collage emphasizes a particular shape within the overall collage. You'll learn how to define an image by piecing it as an individual collage and then applying it to a background. By creating the separate collage shape, you have the opportunity to look at a variety of backgrounds before permanently committing to them.

But don't get hemmed into creating art within a frame—try using the frame to make the art! Wood boxes and shadow frames are great supports in collage art, don't be afraid to collage on all sides.

No. n	Sq. n²	Cube n³	Sq. Root √n	Cube Root ∛n	n	n²	n³	√n	∛n

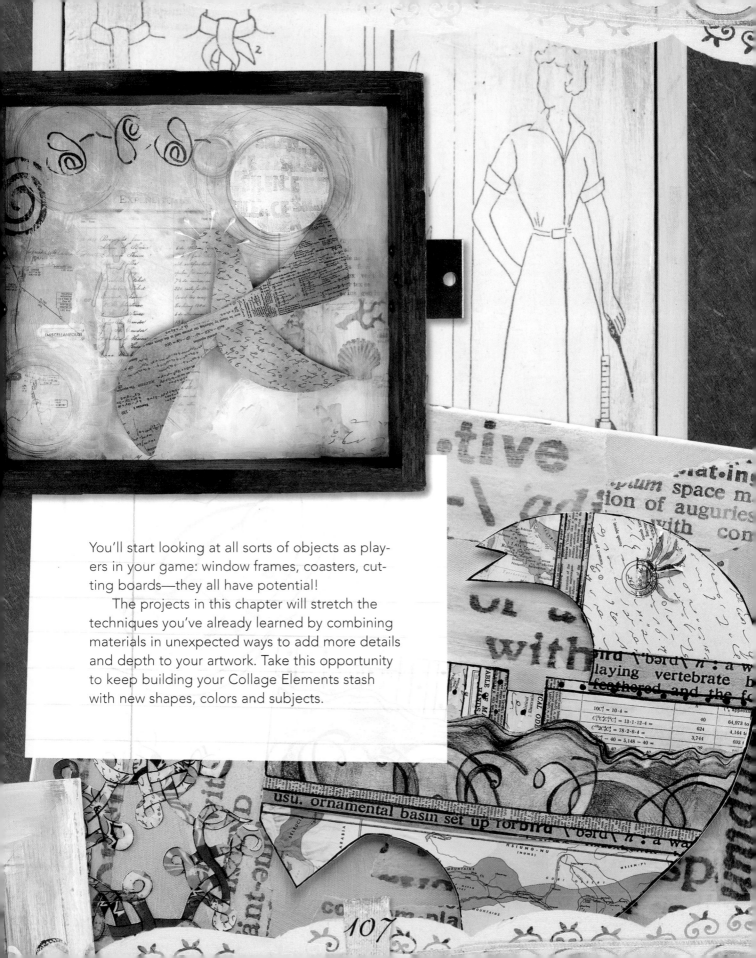

You'll start looking at all sorts of objects as players in your game: window frames, coasters, cutting boards—they all have potential!

The projects in this chapter will stretch the techniques you've already learned by combining materials in unexpected ways to add more details and depth to your artwork. Take this opportunity to keep building your Collage Elements stash with new shapes, colors and subjects.

No. n	Sq. n²	Cube n³	Sq. Root √n	Cube Root ³√n	n	n²	n³	√n	³√n

BANDANA

Look closely at this piece. Do you see the image on the glass? Isn't it a nice surprise? Shadow frames are the perfect platform to use transparency sheets. Repeated images across the inside of the box and out on the edge give the piece rhythm.

MATERIALS

sandpaper

wood-frame shadow box

acrylic paint in rose, orange, yellow, yellow oxide and white

palette

paintbrushes

matte medium

pages from vintage math book

scissors

craft knife

cutting mat

putty knife

images of women

images of flowers

pencil

color copier

copy paper

window cleaner

paper towels

COLLAGE ELEMENTS

Transparency Art or image of woman's profile on transparency sheet with adhesive back

1. Paint shadow box

Using the sandpaper, smooth the surface of the frame.

Pour the acrylic paints onto the palette. Paint the box and frame with the rose acrylic paint and allow to dry. Using a clean, dry brush, paint the box and frame with the orange, yellow and yellow oxide paints, blending them as desired. Allow the paints to dry.

Thin down some white acrylic paint with an equal amount of the matte medium. Using a clean brush, lightly brush the mixture over the frame.

2. Collage paper to inside of box

Using a page from a vintage math book, cut a strip large enough to cover the bottom inside of the box (this example is approximately 3" × 8" [8cm × 20cm]).

Apply matte medium to the inside of the box and position the strip, wrapping it around the edges on the inside walls. Use the craft knife to trim any excess paper.

Tip

If you find it difficult to get the paper to lay neatly in the corners and edges, use a putty knife to get into those tight spaces.

3. Blend paper with paint

Using the paintbrush, apply a light coat of paint and matte medium mixture over the collage paper. Allow the paint to dry.

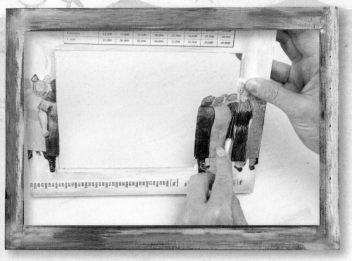

5. Collage frame

Use matte medium to add strips of math pages to the frame and layer on any desired images. Use the craft knife to trim as needed.

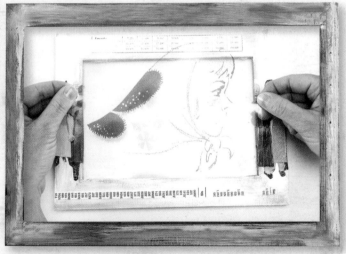

4. Add images of flowers and women

Apply matte medium to the inside of the box to adhere the images of the flowers and women as desired, making sure to wrap the edges on the inside of the box. Use the pencil to outline the women and flowers, if desired.

Tip

You may want to consider using color copies of women or try using multiple copies of the same woman repeated as the background for a different look.

6. Apply transparency art on glass

Search your Collage Elements to see if you have transparency art you'd like to use on the glass. If not, copy an image of a woman's profile on the clear adhesive sheet. Cut the sheet to the size of the glass.

Clean the glass with some window cleaner and a paper towel (spray the window cleaner on the paper towel, not directly on the glass). Allow the glass to dry.

Apply the transparency image to the glass. Smooth down by laying a piece of paper over the transparency for protection and gently pressing with your fingers.

Reassemble the shadow-box frame.

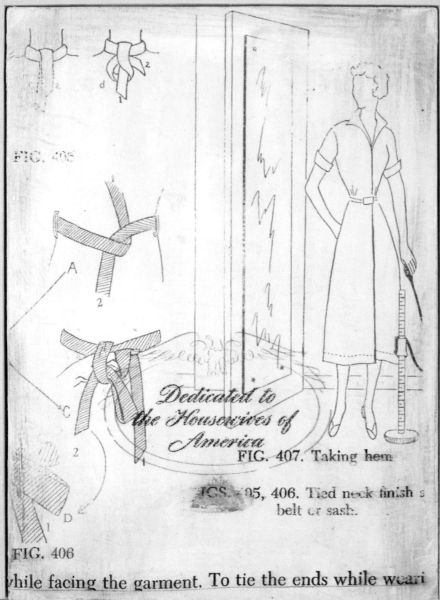

FIG. 405

A

C

2

D

1

FIG. 406

Dedicated to the Housewives of America

FIG. 407. Taking hem

IGS. 405, 406. Tied neck finish s
belt or sash.

hile facing the garment. To tie the ends while wear

FIGURE #407

I consider this piece a hybrid interactive with dimension. Slide the door open and view the image within. I loved pulling from the Collage Elements—using Rub-On Transfers, Sticker Paper art and Vellum Elements to create this piece of art. Take a look at your stash and find something that speaks to you.

sandpaper

small unfinished wood box with lid

acrylic paint in yellow, gray and white

palette

paintbrushes

graphic images of sewing instructions

tracing paper

scissors

matte medium

putty knife

craft knife

Double Tack Mounting Film

image of woman printed on Kodak Premium Photo Paper for the inside of box

embroidery scissors

COLLAGE ELEMENTS

Rub-on Transfers

Sticker Paper art (optional)

Vellum Elements (optional)

1. Prepare box

Using the sandpaper, smooth all sides, inside and out, of the box and all sides of the lid.

Pour the acrylic paints onto the palette. Paint the box and lid with the yellow paint. Let the paint dry. Using a clean, dry brush, paint selected areas of the box with gray and white paint, using quick brushstrokes.

Copy the graphic images of sewing instructions onto the tracing paper. Cut strips to fit the sides and back of the box and the top of the lid. Using the matte medium, adhere the tracing paper to the bottom of the box.

2. Smooth tracing paper

Use the putty knife to smooth down any wrinkles or bubbles. Allow the matte medium to dry.

Apply the remaining pieces of tracing paper in this fashion until all sides of the box are covered. Use the craft knife to trim excess paper as needed.

3. Apply rub-on transfer

Choose a rub-on transfer from your Collage Elements and add it to the lid of the box. Do you feel your art needs more? Pull some stickers or images printed on vellum from your stash of Collage Elements to complete the look you desire.

Using the sandpaper, lightly rub the transfers to give them a distressed look.

4. Adhere woman's image to inside of box

Apply Double Tack Mounting Film to the photograph of the woman. Use the embroidery scissors to cut out the image. Apply the image to the inside of the box.

Tip

If you plan on handling the box, I recommend spraying it with a matte seal spray for protection.

SMALL TALK

"Mind Chatter" is what I call the nonstop thoughts that can run through my mind as I try to sleep. You know what I am referring to—the never-ending list of things to do.

Small Talk is my visual representation of this thought process. This piece was fun to create—the background is comprised of graffiti and random thoughts. Give it a try; let this art release your thoughts and turn them into art! How are you going to fit everything in your head onto this small canvas? I say be selective and choose only two or three topics. Working in smaller sizes can sometimes help eliminate being overwhelmed by big ideas.

If you want to put your spin on this idea, pull out your stash of Collage Elements and spontaneously add them to the background: stickers, Rub-On Transfers, transparency sheets—whatever floats your boat! Express yourself without editing and reflect your "mind chatter."

MATERIALS

vintage illustrations of children (for the bodies)

color copier

copy paper

proportion wheel

Double Tack Mounting Film

white cover stock paper

scissors

oil pastels

original drawings by children (for the heads)

acrylic paints in blue, green, purple and white

palette

paintbrushes

8" × 10" (20cm × 25cm) gallery wrapped canvas

fine-tip markers in black and blue

alphabet stencil with 1" (3cm) letters (optional)

sandpaper

self-adhesive foam pop-ups

Tip

Have fun with your version of this artwork! Write down the silly and crazy things that float through your head. Use your creativity and incorporate shapes and styles of letters. Explore different ways to position the letters, including a mix of handwriting and stenciling.

1. Prepare images

Make black-and-white copies of the vintage illustrations. Reduce or enlarge as needed to fit the canvas.

Add Double Tack Mounting Film to the back of the images and adhere them to a sheet of cover stock. Using the scissors, cut the images out.

With the oil pastels, color in the body of your images as desired.

2. Add heads

Make color copies of the children's drawings. You will only be using the head on each of the figures. The size of the head and the body need to complement one another, so reduce or enlarge the images as needed. Use the proportion wheel to aid in these calculations.

Add Double Tack Mounting Film to the backs of the heads. Using the scissors, cut the images out.

Peel the backing of the Double Tack Mounting Film and adhere each head on top of the existing head of each figure.

3. Add graffiti and stencil

Paint the canvas blue, green, purple and white, blending the colors to your desired look. Allow the paint to dry.

Using markers, and stencils if desired, write thoughts and phrases on the canvas. Fill in any stencil letters with oil pastels.

When all your graffiti is complete, scribble lines over the entire canvas with the oil pastels. Use the sandpaper to blend the oil pastels into the background. With a clean brush, remove grit from the canvas.

If desired, add more items from your Collage Elements stash to make the piece your own.

4. Add pop-up images

Adhere the foam pop-ups to the back sides of the images. Position the images on the canvas as desired.

Mind Chatter

While I love the intimate feel of Small Talk, this larger piece definitely has great impact. The size alone forces the viewer to smile at the whimsy of each character, while encouraging to come closer to read the background graffiti.

118

SOUNDS OF SILENCE

Some days I crave the sounds of silence. No radio, no television, nothing—just the sound of my studio, breathing in and out. Turn off all noisemakers, even the phone, look around your studio and start to make art. Gather a combination of Collage Elements, vintage papers, paint, stencils and rubber stamps to help create a soothing piece of art.

MATERIALS

2 pieces of 16" × 20" (41cm × 51cm) 100-lb. vellum finish bristol paper

vintage imagery and illustrations

vintage book pages of shorthand, maps, math and ledgers

matte medium

stencil template (I used a stencil from *Fun with Family Stencils* by Dover Books)

colored pencils

putty knife

palette

acrylic paint in yellow oxide, yellow, blue, green and white

paintbrushes

sandpaper

pencil

sketch paper

Double Tack Mounting Film

craft knife

cutting mat

two-sided tape

pearl embellishments

self-adhesive foam pop-ups

canvas paper

scissors

rubber stamps of your choice

black ink pad

7" × 16" (18cm × 41cm) shadow-box frame

staple gun

COLLAGE ELEMENTS

Altered Book Pages

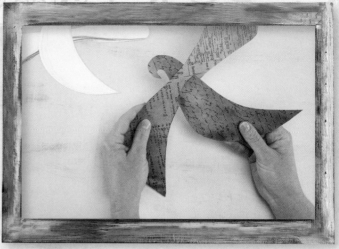

1. Collage background

Create a collage background on a piece of bristol paper. Tear different sized strips of papers and apply to the sheet of bristol paper with matte medium. Allow the matte medium to dry. For added interest, use a stencil and trace with a pencil into the background. Use colored pencils to color in the stencil. Smooth down the collage paper with the putty knife if needed.

Prepare your paint palette with small amounts of both yellows, blue, green, white and matte medium. Mix the matte medium into each color before applying to the background. Brush strokes of paint randomly throughout the background, allow the paint to dry. Distress the painted surface with sandpaper.

2. Create and assemble bird

Using the sketch paper and pencil, draw an abstract image of a bird. The bird is composed of two separate pieces—the wing and the body. Use the sketch to make two separate Shape Cut Outs of the wings and the body on the second piece of bristol paper.

Fit an Altered Book Page to the body of the bird and the wings, using two different page designs to give them contrast. Apply Double Tack Mounting Film to the Altered Book Page and adhere them to the bird body and wing. Place the pieces facedown and trim the excess paper with a craft knife.

Cut a single slit in the middle section of the wings and slide the wings down the body of the bird, securing the back of the wings with a small piece of two-sided tape.

3. Add bird to canvas

To add the pearls to the head of the bird, adhere two-sided tape to the back of the head and gently press the pearls into place.

Add the pop-up adhesive dots or squares to the back of the bird. Position the bird on the background and press gently to adhere it to the background.

Tip

For this project, I chose to reinforce the theme by adding the word "silence," but you can use any stamp. This particular stamp is made up of adhesive rubber sheets and separate wood blocks. There are so many types and styles of rubber stamps out there; the options for your own artwork are virtually endless!

4. Embellish sun

Trace a 4" (10cm) circle on the canvas paper. Paint inside the circle with yellow paint. Allow the paint to dry, and cut out the circle.

Place the sun shape on a piece of scrap paper. Using a rubber stamp of your choice and black ink, stamp across the painted canvas circle. Let the ink dry.

5. Embellish background

Use the pop-up adhesive to adhere the canvas circle piece to the background.

Embellish the background further by adding more rubber-stamp designs. Using the pencil, draw lines and circles to enhance your art.

6. Mount art to a shadow frame

Pick up the shadow frame and determine the front and back of the frame. Position the art facedown on the back of the frame. Using the staple gun, secure the artwork to the frame. Trim away any excess paper from the frame with the craft knife.

JOIN THE WOMEN'S CLUB

When I came across the image of this woman, her look was so intriguing that my first thought was, "a retro Mona Lisa." Postwar life for women in the 1950s was considered modern, with new and fancy appliances, gadgets and, especially, the influence of Hollywood.

My intent was to showcase the mystery of this young woman, along with the unity women were feeling at this time through women's clubs and other social groups. This is emphasized in the vintage postage stamp sitting above her hand. The juxtaposition of the piece is the subtle background of graphics with scenes of a woman clearly in distress, contradicted by the line "simple beauty."

Tip

The use of pop-up foam adhesives in your artwork is a great technique to bring the viewer into your piece. Creating dimension within a two-dimensional surface allows you to showcase a particular image and idea.

MATERIALS

comic or graphic illustration

color copier

3 sheets of manila drawing paper 8½" × 11" (22cm × 28cm) (to print comics for background)

iron

fusible webbing

12" × 17" (30cm × 43cm) piece of chipboard

colored tissue paper

scissors

matte medium

putty knife

purchased rub-on letters (the word "beauty")

burnisher

sandpaper

paintbrushes

image of retro woman

8½" × 11" (22cm × 28cm) sheet of sticker paper

8½" × 11" (22cm × 28cm) sheet of white cover stock

oil pastels

paper towels

2" × 2" (5cm × 5cm) piece of chipboard

textured kraft paper

wax paper

heavy book

vintage postage stamp

self-adhesive foam pop-ups

small flat-backed crystal

fine-tip black marker

metal ruler

14" × 19" (36cm × 48cm) shadow box frame

staple gun

craft knife

cutting mat

COLLAGE ELEMENTS

Rub-On Transfers of text (the phrase "simple beauty")

2. Apply comic strips to background

With the third copied sheet of manila paper, cut out strips of the comics. Use matte medium to adhere the strips of the comics or graphics across the top of the background. Smooth down with a putty knife, if needed.

1. Prepare background

Make three copies of the comics or graphic illustrations on the manila drawing paper. Iron the fusible webbing onto the back of two of the copies. Fuse these two pages onto the piece of 12" × 17" (30cm × 43cm) chipboard.

Iron the fusible webbing onto the colored tissue paper. Lay the tissue paper on the background and use the iron to fuse it to the background.

3. Add Rub-On Transfers

Use Rub-On Transfers, either purchased or from your Collage Elements, to enhance the theme. If using purchased transfers, follow the manufacturer's instructions.

(For this piece, I used letters from the set Urban Letters by Letraset to spell out the word "beauty." The phrase "simple beauty" came from my Collage Elements stash.)

4. Distress background

Using the sandpaper, gently distress the background, including the Rub-On Transfers. When you are satisfied with the look, brush off any grit with a clean brush.

5. Create sticker paper image

Make a Sticker Paper image of the woman (see page 33). Adhere the sticker paper to a sheet of the white cover stock paper.

Color in and embellish the image with the oil pastels. Use the paper towels to blend the oil pastels. Use the scissors to cut out the image.

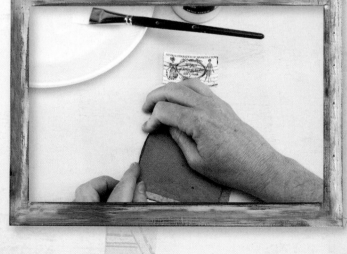

6. Create vintage stamp piece

Using the matte medium as the adhesive, cover the 2" × 2" (5cm × 5cm) piece of chipboard with the textured kraft paper. Fold edges of the craft paper to the back of the chipboard for a neater look. Allow the matte medium to dry.

Tip

To keep the chipboard from curling or warping after the matte medium has been applied, place the chipboard faceup on a hard surface, cover it with wax paper and put a heavy book on top. This will weigh the chipboard down while it is drying, preventing it from warping.

8. Adhere images to background

Add the pop-up adhesives to the back of the woman and place the image on the background. Use matte medium to adhere the flat-backed crystal as an earring.

Add the pop-up adhesives to the back of the vintage-stamp piece. Slide the small square under the woman's finger and adhere it to the background.

7. Embellish vintage-stamp piece

Use the matte medium to adhere the vintage postage stamp to the front of the piece created in step 6. Allow the matte medium to dry.

Use Rub-On Transfers, either purchased or from your Collage Elements, to enhance the theme. Repeating a letter, alternating letters or turning them upside down or sideways creates a cool design.

Embellish the piece with oil pastels.

Tip

Because of the rarity of vintage postage stamps, you may want to make a color copy of the original stamp.

9. Embellish with black marker

Using the black marker and ruler, plan your lines, linking the images within the composition to one another.

10. Affix art to shadow-box frame

Pick up the shadow frame and determine the front and back. Position the art facedown on the back of the frame. Using the staple gun, affix the artwork to the frame. Trim any excess paper or chipboard away from the frame with the craft knife.

Detail of *Join the Women's Club*

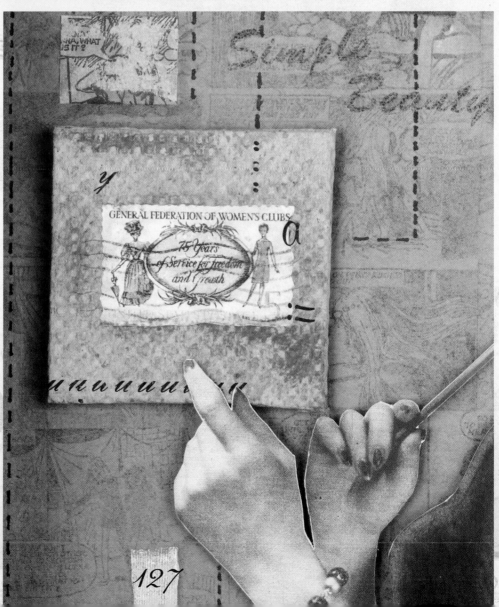

CONTEMPLATE BIRD

MATERIALS

acrylic paint in blue and white

palette

paintbrushes

12" × 16" (30cm × 41cm) gallery wrapped canvas

dictionary page "contemplate" entry

color copier

proportion wheel

copy paper

matte medium

putty knife

pencil

11" × 14" (28cm × 36cm) piece of 100-lb. bristol paper, with a vellum finish

11" × 14" (28cm × 36cm) sheet of Double Tack Mounting Film

fine-tip black marker

vintage book pages from shorthand and math books

pieces of unfinished artwork, sketches or drawings

vintage maps

scissors

craft knife

cutting mat

vintage postage stamp

3 mirrors 1" × 2" (3cm × 5cm)

COLLAGE ELEMENTS

Altered Book Pages

Textile featuring a symbol

I have an old paperback dictionary I like to use for collage projects because the slightly aged pages add wonderful qualities to my art. The design the words make on the page are art in themselves. When developing this piece, the word "contemplate" jumped out at me. I am forever contemplating art; what about you?

Take a look at the symbol in the lower left corner of the artwork. I pulled it from my stash of Collage Elements: It was appropriate for this project because it is derived from an ancient symbol meaning "to contemplate." See what unique imagery you can come up with while digging around in your stash of Collage Elements.

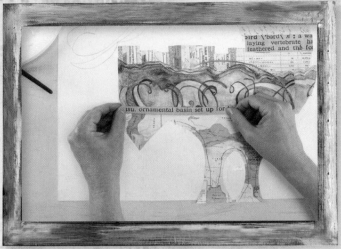

2. Collage bird image

Sketch a simple shape of a bird on a piece of bristol paper. Trace over the final design with the fine-tip black marker. Adhere Double Tack Mounting Film to the back.

Take a look at your bird sketch and decide which areas you want to define.

Layer the assorted papers onto the sketch, cutting where needed to fit. For those areas that are hard to fit (in this case, the bird's legs), add more paper than is needed and sketch the original lines onto the added paper. You will use these lines later to cut out the shape.

Use a clean paintbrush and matte medium to adhere the papers onto the sketch. Use the putty knife to smooth the papers.

1. Prepare background

Pour the acrylic paints onto the palette. Using the paintbrush, paint the canvas light blue, including all four sides. Allow the paint to dry.

Find the word "contemplate" in the dictionary; cut out and manipulate it at different sizes on a copier. You will need several copies.

Tear strips of the copies of the word "contemplate" and layer the paper using matte medium. Use the putty knife to smooth down the paper and eliminate bubbles.

Tip

Select a variety of papers and don't forget to use your own artwork. Incorporating fragments such as unfinished drawings or sketches gives the collage a degree of personality.

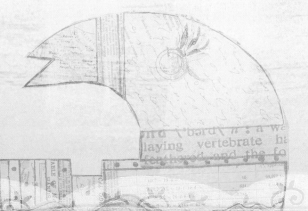

3. Layer to create bird's tail

Continue layering paper on the sketch until you have completed the collage. Allow the matte medium to dry.

4. Cut cut bird collage

Using the scissors and craft knife (for detailed areas), cut out the bird and tail.

6. Embellish details

Enhance the bird by adding details. I have selected a vintage postage stamp for the eye.

7. Outline with black marker

Using a fine-tip black marker, outline the bird's shape and embellish within the bird's body. I drew lines and circles to define areas.

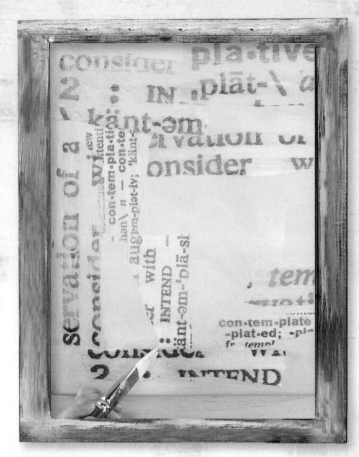

9. Adhere bird to background

Peel the backing off the Double Tack Mounting Film, position the bird on the canvas and adhere. Once you have completed all collage applications, flip the canvas over and apply weight to the back. Allow to set for an hour.

8. Blend collage paper with paint

Using a mixture of the light blue acrylic paint and matte medium, brush a layer over the paper to help blend the paper with the background. Allow to dry.

10. Add symbol and mirrors

Embellish the artwork with a symbol from your Collage Elements stash. Add the mirrors by brushing a coat of matte medium to the back of the mirror and gently pressing down on the canvas. Once all the mirrors are applied, allow the art to set flat, undisturbed, for one hour.

HEAD IN THE CLOUDS

Using a vintage boys' magazine seemed ideal to collage this graphic illustration of two boys. The diagrams and charts convert easily to shirts and pants. Look for compatible materials when you are developing your collage. Think about how collage pieces can translate into images.

MATERIALS

acrylic paint in blue and white

matte medium

palette

vintage book pages

11" × 14" (28cm × 36cm) bristol paper

putty knife

paintbrushes

graphic image

medium-tip black marker

images of two boys

vintage boys' magazine illustrations, graphs and diagrams

color copier

scissors

Double Tack Mounting Film

pencil

craft knife

cutting mat

vintage magazine illustration (for tree branch)

image of bird

COLLAGE ELEMENTS
Altered Book Page

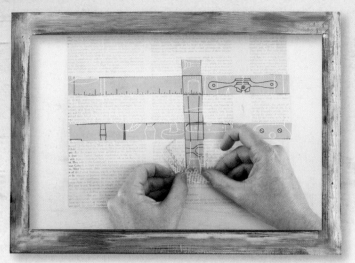

1. Collage and paint background

Adhere book pages to the bristol paper using matte medium; use the putty knife to smooth out and remove bubbles. Pour the matte medium and acrylic paints onto the palette. Cover the entire surface. Allow the matte medium to dry. Paint background with light blue acrylic paint, set aside to dry.

To make a fence, cut three strips from an illustration and adhere them with matte medium. Cut grass out of an Altered Book Page. Using the matte medium, adhere to the fence post at the bottom. Use the putty knife to smooth down paper, if needed. Allow the matte medium to dry.

2. Cut shapes for boys' images

Make two to three black-and-white copies of the two figures and cut figures into sections (head, shirt, arms, pants, shoes, etc.). You may divide the figures into as many sections as you desire.

Look at the magazine pages and decide which will be the head, shirt, arms, pants, shoes, etc. Apply Double Tack Mounting Film to the back of the magazine selections. Trace their corresponding shapes and use the scissors to cut them out.

3. Assemble figures on background

Adhere the figures to the background. Remember to work from back to front when assembling the figure (for example, the shoes will be adhered before the pants). Use the craft knife to help peel backing from the Double Tack Mounting Film.

4. Embellish shapes

Adhere Double Tack Mounting Film to the back of a small rectangle of a vintage magazine illustration. Using the scissors, cut a branch shape out and adhere it to upper left corner of the background. Place Double Tack Mounting Film on the back of the bird. Cut out the bird and adhere it on top of branch.

Using the medium-tip black marker, outline the shapes, draw in lines and define areas of the figures. Make the figures as personable as you desire.

Typecast

People often ask me how I select a particular book or book page for my collage work. What is it I'm looking for? Usually it is the graphics or quality of print within the book, but sometimes, like in reference to this project, it is an emotional connection to the material.

I came across a vintage typing manual and immediately laughed out loud. Why? Oh, the many, many hours spent in typing class, trying endlessly to type (with accuracy) as fast as I could. Therefore, I couldn't resist the book and using the cover image for a collage piece. The bright orange and flowing line of the words felt perfect for an evening dress on my retro woman. When something engages your emotion, go with it, trust it and make it a part of your collage!

ROYAL BIRD

Peacocks are such regal birds with their beautiful colors and spanning feathers. I wanted to create a piece of art that was similar but more understated than *Contemplate Bird* (page 128). I found a map with intricate graphics to use for my bird and used pastel paper to introduce color. Bringing in metallic gold pushed the bird into a royal state. What colors, images or texture emphasize royalty to you? Look at the shape of your bird; how can you express elegance?

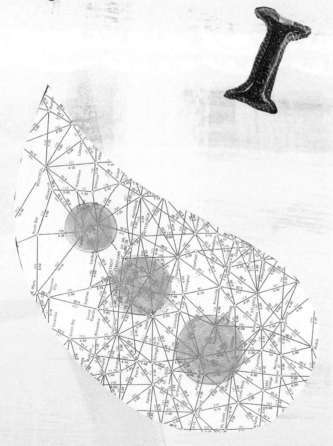

MATERIALS

acrylic paint in black, burnt sienna, burnt umber, gold metallic

matte medium

palette

12" × 16" (30cm × 41cm) gallery wrapped canvas

paintbrushes

torn pieces of vintage letters

putty knife

2 vintage postage stamps

pastel paper in assorted colors

vintage maps

scissors

color copier

pencil

sketch paper

text (for eye, legs and band)

proportion wheel

craft knife

cutting mat

circle template

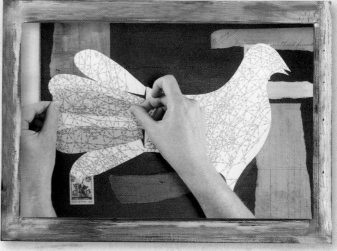

1. Layer paper on canvas

Pour the acrylic paints and matte medium onto the palette. Paint the canvas black, including all four sides. Set aside to dry. Once the canvas has dried, tear strips of paper and begin layering the paper using matte medium. Use the putty knife to smooth down the paper and eliminate bubbles. Add vintage stamps as embellishments. To help blend the starkness of the paper and stamps onto the black background, add a small amount of matte medium to a neutral-colored paint (I used burnt umber and burnt sienna) and brush over the entire canvas.

2. Add bird shape

Cut three sheets of yellow pastel paper, one sheet of tan, and one sheet of buff to 8½" × 11" (22cm × 28cm). Make copies of the map onto these sheets of paper.

Sketch a simple shape of a bird and use this sketch to make a template. Use the template and trace the bird's body and wing onto the yellow paper, and cut out. With the remaining papers, trace and cut out the feathers, making the feathers slightly different shapes and sizes. You will need approximately four feathers from each color of paper.

Using the matte medium and a clean brush, assemble the bird on the background (it is important you use a clean brush because you do not want to get paint on the bird). When adding the feathers, alternate different colors and shapes.

4. Draw circles

On the bird's wing, use a circle template to trace three circles (each one a different size).

3. Add letters and text

With the copier, enlarge a band of text and letters for the bird's legs (I) and eye (S), and copy them onto a sheet of tan pastel paper. Cut out the band. The size should cover where the feathers meet the bird's body. Cut out the letters for the legs and eye.

Use the matte medium to adhere the band of text over the area where the bird's body and feathers meet, hiding the seam lines. Adhere the individual letters to their appropriate spots. If needed, use the blade of the craft knife to gently position the letters. If you desire, continue to embellish with more text and letters.

5. Embellish with metallic paint

Enhance the bird with gold metallic paint. Fill in the circles on the wing and outline the feathers and legs.

Resources

Grafix
www.grafixarts.com
Rub-Onz transfer film, Double Tack Mounting Film

Avery
www.avery.com
Sticker paper

Color-aid paper
www.coloraid.com
Color-aid paper

Dover Publications
www.doverpublications.com
stencil books

Inspirational Publications

Mornings Like This: Found Poems
(Harper Perrenial, 1996) by Annie Dillard

Kaleidoscope: Ideas & Projects to Spark Your Creativity (North Light Books, 2007) by Suzanne Simanaitis

Exhibition 36: Mixed-Media Demonstrations + Explorations (North Light Books, 2008) by Susan Tuttle

Craft books and magazines from the 1930s to present

cloth paper scissors magazine
www.quiltingarts.com/cpsmag/cpshome.html

Wallpaper* magazine
www.wallpaper.com

Inspiring Artists

Michael Mew
www.michaelmewstudio.com

Katie Kendrick
www.katiekendrick.com

Michel Keck
www.michelkeck.com

Anna Corba
www.annacorbastudio.com

Jennifer Davis
www.jenniferdavisart.com

Further Inspiration

Frist Center for the Visual Arts, Nashville, Tennessee
www.fristcenter.org

Art Institute of Chicago, Chicago, Illinois
www.artic.edu

MoMA, New York City, New York
www.moma.org

Your local art museum

141

Index

Get more inspiration and instruction from these North Light Books

Collage Fusion
by Alma de la Melena Cox

Fuse vibrantly colored fabric and wood as you discover "telamedera," a new approach to collage. Wood becomes your canvas as you learn to use a wood-burning tool and mixed media elements, including stencil work, dimensional paint, fabric and personal imagery, to bring new art to life. Whether you're a quilter, painter, scrapbooker or completely new to the craft world, the ten projects and twenty techniques in *Collage Fusion* will ignite the fires of your own creativity.

ISBN 13: 978-1-60061-330-2
ISBN-10: 1-60061-330-6
128 pages, paperback, Z2973

Creative Awakenings
by Sherri Gaynor

What if you could unlatch the doors to your heart and allow yourself to explore hopes and dreams that you haven't visited for a very long time? *Creative Awakenings* is the key to opening those doors. You'll learn how to create your own Book-of-Dreams Journal and a variety of mixed-media techniques to use within it. A tear-out Transformation Deck will aid you in setting your intentions. You'll also get inspiration from twelve artists who share their own experiences and artwork created with the Art of Intention process.

ISBN 13: 978-1-60061-115-5
ISBN-10: 1-60061-115-X
144 pages, paperback, Z2122

Image Transfer Workshop
by Darlene Olivia McElroy and Sandra Duran Wilson

Learn 35 transfer techniques (complete with finished art examples) that cover everything from basic tape and gel medium transfers to much more advanced techniques. McElroy's and Wilson's troubleshooting fixes will even enable you to work with your transfers that don't quite live up to expectations. *Image Transfer Workshop* provides a quick reference and examples of art using a variety of techniques that will inspire you to go beyond single transfer applications.

ISBN 13: 978-1-60061-160-5
ISBN-10: 1-60061-160-5
128 pages, paperback, Z2509

These and other fine North Light Books are available at your local craft retailer, bookstore or online supplier, or visit us online at www.mycraftivitystore.com.